Yeah
But,
Children
Need...

Yeah But, Children Need...

By
Karen L. Rancourt

SCHENKMAN PUBLISHING COMPANY
TWO CONTINENTS PUBLISHING GROUP, LTD
CAMBRIDGE — NEW YORK

72111

Copyright ©1978

Schenkman Publishing Company, Inc.
3 Mt. Auburn Place
Cambridge, Massachusetts 02138

Library of Congress Cataloging in Publication Data
Rancourt, Karen.
Yeah but, children need...
1. Children—Management   2. Child development.
I.   Title.
HQ769.R19   649′.1   77-18631
ISBN 0-8467-0451-X

With love and gratitude
To my Mother and Father,
Elia and Arthur Logozzo

Contents

Contents

Preface

EVERYDAY ACTIVITIES allow for informal group discussions: at the supermarket, the cocktail party, the kaffee-klatsch. The one experience common to many members of such groups is that of dealing with children. It is not unusual for one of the group to discuss something new about child-rearing—a different solution tried or read about; nor is it unusual for another to be all but jumping up and down waiting for the speaker to pause so that he/she can refute what is being said. A standard opening line is often, "Yeah but, children need...."

Somewhere back in my student teaching days I remember being told, "Never smile at the kids before December." My later work in supervising student teachers taught me that I was not alone in receiving this message. The month may vary; some instructors will say that smiling is taboo until January and some of the more liberal ones will designate November as the ideal time to do the smile thing. The group of student teachers will invariably titter and ho-ho knowingly at this decree. The message is that it requires several months for the teacher to establish himself/herself as the one in charge. Occasionally a student teacher will question this with a well-thought-out rebuttal, and the instructor can be counted on to begin his/her reply, gently of course, with, "Ah yes, but children need...."

The "Yeah but, children need..." phenomenon affects many of us—educators, parents, baby-sitters. Everyone who interacts with children has some very definite ideas about child-rearing. This is all well and good. There should be intent and purpose guiding our involvements with children. But what is needed is some re-evaluation of these goals and objectives, especially in light of recent research which suggests very strong implications about children's potentialities, capabilities, and needs.

In the past such appraisals may have been difficult for the average individual who either was not aware of research findings, or did not know where or how to go about studying them in relation to his/her children. The findings and suggestions of pertinent research only slowly filter down to the general public, mainly via consumer publications. There is a problem with disseminating information in this manner.

Those who most need access to research findings, suggestions, and implications are often forced to deal with the information piecemeal; that is, they read an isolated article about "Children and Punishment" or "Your Child and Bedtime." Because they are often not exposed to total philosophies or theories, defensiveness sets in: "What So-and-So is saying sounds good, but children need...!" This is understandable and partially helps explain why different approaches to working with children are seldom applied.

People often finish off the phrase, "Yeah but, children need...", with "authority," "discipline," "morals and values," or "to know their limitations." I wrote this book to scrutinize these pat replies. During the past few years it became very apparent to me that traditional or unquestioned ideas about childhood had become culturally imbued and new or different ideas were being disregarded or supposedly refuted in the name of "Yeah but, children need...." I felt that it was important for someone to present an up-to-date survey of relevant research in order to help all adults who interact with children understand the multi-faceted dimensions of children's needs. Further, I felt it imperative that this discussion of theory and research be readable and comprehensible: no mysterious *chi-squares* or other baffling statistics; no psychological jargon and terminology; and no vague references to related research to confuse the reader further. I saw a need for a straightforward discussion of important research and its relevance to everyday situations.

After years of complaining and saying "Why doesn't someone fulfill this need?", I assigned the task to myself. My intent was to write a book that would provide today's parent and educator with a cohesive presentation of the extensive research which has affected the evolution of child-rearing techniques, so that each individual could effectively question and even possibly change his/her own methods of interacting with children.

The first five chapters begin with a short dialogue between two people. Hopefully, in many cases, the reader will be flooded with *déjà vu.* "Yes! Yes! I remember some adult saying that to me when I was a child," or "Oh yes! I have said that exact same thing to a child." This conversation is used to set the scene for the content in each chapter. Following this is an intertwining of related research and examples from my own personal experiences. Happily, I am able to relate incidents and experiences which cause me warm and glowing memories. Not so happily but realistically, I also relate anecdotes which leave me with feelings of "Dammit! I wish I hadn't said or done that." Finally, each chapter contains my reflections as a Person, Parent, and Educator.

I had a bit of a struggle in deciding what to do with Chapter 1, "A Historical Framework." I felt it was important to establish a context of historical background to show how previously unquestioned views of children have developed, but at the same time I did not want a reader to begin this chapter and conclude "Oh. This is a history book." I have not written a history book, but rather, I have included a historical perspective. I realize that this chapter may not be of interest to everyone and my feelings will not be hurt if a reader chooses to begin with Chapter 2. Chapters 2-5 deal with four needs attributed to children. Chapters 6-8 deal specifically with the process of change and ways of experimenting with different approaches in interacting with children.

I learned a lot and had a good time writing this book. May each reader learn a lot and have a good time reading it!

Acknowledgments

I would like to express my appreciation to Mary S. O'Connor and Linda Lee Sutton. I will always treasure their friendship, help, and support. My editor at Schenkman Publishing Company, Kathy Schlivek, deserves a special note of gratitude for her suggestions, guidance, and expert editing. And a special thank you to my husband, Gary, for his cooperation, confidence, and ability to retain his sense of humor!

1

*"But many readers may not be interested in the
history of how the concept of childhood evolved."*

*"Then they have the option of going right on to
Chapter 2. But I really think that to appreciate fully
the impact of this book, most readers will want and
need*

A Historical Framework

THE IDEA OF childhood and what is believed to be the nature of
children have become almost sanctified in our society. We treat
many of our conceptions about children as if they must be defined
and implemented in one way. It seems also that we have polarized
many of our ways of interacting with and viewing children. "It is
right" to do such and such with children and "It is wrong" to do
something else. However, historical perspective shows that
approaches to living with children have in fact changed through
the centuries. It is important to note what these changes have
been, and to understand how they have reflected different social,
economic, and political needs. This historical perspective helps
us understand how some of our own ideas have developed, and
provides us with an impetus to question some of them. It is
reassuring to know that one is not tampering with the deity after
all!

Philippe Aries' excellent book *Centuries of Childhood* depicts
the history of childhood. Aries presented his work according to
topics—art, education, family-life, etc., but I summarize his work
here chronologically and highlight and interpret data relevant to
the development of child-rearing processes, while restraining
myself from commenting on criticisms put forth by some
reviewers.

CHILDREN: MINIATURE ADULTS

The art of the thirteenth century shows that although the Infant Jesus was a common subject, children were not considered appropriate subjects to be painted. In those few works where children were depicted they were always shown as miniature adults. Aries suggests that at this time there probably was no place for childhood as we know it. It was most likely considered a transitional stage of short duration. From a medieval text:

> The first age is childhood when the teeth are planted, and this age begins when the child is born and lasts until seven, and in this age that which is born is called an infant, which is as good as saying not talking, because in this age it cannot talk well or form its words perfectly, for its teeth are not yet arranged firmly or implanted (Aries, p. 21).

The idea of childhood is suggested but limited to a physiological delineation.

During the thirteenth century the law of primogeniture spread, especially among the nobility. Exclusive right of inheritance for the eldest son replaced joint ownership. In the economic and social framework, having a child of a particular gender took on important significance. Even today there is special reverence for first-born sons. This helps us understand the unfortunate but common reaction when a first-born child is female, "Oh well, maybe you'll have a boy next time." Boy-babies were then and are sometimes still considered more valuable than girl-babies.

In the fourteenth century children are depicted in groups with other children and adults. Apparently the child of this century interacted freely with adults in all phases of life, in work, and socially. During this time such disciplinary measures as whipping were used on children, designed deliberately to humiliate them; it was felt that this would ensure improved behavior. Whipping was not confined to any one class; rich and poor alike were disciplined in this way.

The idea of the modern family as we know it today began to take shape. Prior to the fourteenth century a wife could assume her husband's vocational responsibilities in his absence, illness, or death. However, for reasons that are not clear, in the 1300s the wife's right to succeed her husband disappeared, which resulted in a lowering of her position—both in the household and in society as a whole. Domestic activities were becoming the wife's exclusive domain, and these included the care of children.

Emphasis shifted in the fifteenth century to education. A particular master worked with a given group of children, the grouping decided on the basis of age. Younger children were educated separately from older. This is significant in that different stages of growth were recognized. The emphasis was on physical growth, but differences in abilities were beginning to be recognized for different age groups.

The "big houses" flourished. In this life style, large houses served as open kinds of communities with families and servants all living together in all parts of the quarters. It was a socially oriented way of life with visitors arriving, unannounced, during all hours of day and night. The concept of privacy was unknown. Children were unquestionably accepted and participated freely in all activities. Even though the presence of children was recognized, Aries suggests that emotional ties and commitments were minimal. The survival rate for children was low, and parents produced many children, largely in the hope that a few might survive; parents just did not get attached to their progeny.

This lack of feeling towards children was gradually to change in the sixteenth century. The paintings of the time included children as a common subject. Many portraits included figures representing children who had died, suggesting the beginning of feelings toward children. For the first time calendars depicting different family scences including the children became popular. Another new phenomenon was the use of individual children as subjects for portraits.

The mode of dress changed. Until this time children had always dressed as adults, but now children, especially boys and upper-class children, were given costumes which were different from what the adults wore. The garb was distinctly for younger folk.

Education became geared primarily to the young. The apprenticeship way of life was changing. To become an apprentice in the past, a child had usually left his own home around the age of seven to live with his master's family while learning his trade. Many of these children never returned home to live. Now the children lived in their natural parents' home while apprenticing. The father was becoming established as the undisputed head of the family; at the same time, the mother's role was reduced almost exclusively to domestic chores. Interestingly, the children of this century had their own right to change masters without obtaining adult permission. This resulted in great rivalry and dissension among the masters, and children eventually had to relinquish this right. It was a right that had slowly and naturally emerged; when it became a recognizable source of difficulty to the adults, the preferences of the young gave way to those of their elders.

In short, a definite concept of childhood emerged during the sixteenth century. Children became a source of amusement and entertainment for adults. New attentions were given to children, and the groundwork was being laid for the day of the child!

The child of the seventeenth century became the artists' favorite model; even in family portraits children were used as focal points. Whereas in the past art had been produced primarily for religious purposes, art was now being produced for decorating private homes. The idea of a private life was depicted in the paintings. Also, there was an interest in nudity in child portraiture.

Toys, which in the past had been designed for and used by both children and adults, were being designed exclusively for infants and young children. These included dolls and knick-knacks. After the ages of three or four, children played the same games as adults. Children were also under pressure to learn musical instruments in order to perform at after-dinner concerts.

Moral teachings became important; it was believed that children had to be cleansed of imperfections. An interest in child psychology thrived; if the behavior of little children was to be corrected, it was first necessary to understand their behavior. Little schools were set up for children ages five to eleven. These schools tended to isolate elementary education and consequently to isolate the children from the adult activities in which they had previously participated so freely. The predominant theme of the time was that society's only salvation was in a good education for all.

Religious organizations became concerned with educating the poor and charity schools opened up. The brothers who ran these schools were considered to be well-qualified and as a result the charity schools became popular among the wealthy. Attraction to these schools by the wealthier classes impeded the further isolation of children. They were still separated from the rest of society by age, but they were not as yet totally sub-categorized by economic or social class.

CHILDREN: WELL-BRED

The idea of the well-bred child spread. In the past children were accepted in an almost complacent way, but now their actions and behavior were a source of concern. Parents were beginning to view children as a reflection of themselves, the start of the "What will other people think?" syndrome. Another popular idea of the seventeenth century was that man's fulfillment came in terms of serving God and his family. Primogeniture was an offensive notion. Each child was entitled to an equal share of family affection. Aries emphasizes that it is difficult to separate changing attitudes toward the family from changing concepts of childhood; the two are interwoven. As the idea of family life and fulfillment became a value, children became more valuable. The big houses were losing their importance, the idea of a private life was growing, and family relationships were becoming more significant.

In terms of attitudes and ideas about childhood, the eighteenth century is important. Many of our present child-rearing attitudes and methods can be traced back to it. During this century everything about the child became a great source of concern. The child became the focus of family life. New scientific strides in the areas of hygiene and physical health were reflected in new attitudes towards children's health. The use of deliberate humiliation as a disciplinary method diminished. Childhood was still viewed as a time of weakness, but corporal punishment was considered inappropriate.

A vitally important idea took root at this time, one that would become entrenched during the nineteenth century and mold much of our thinking in the twentieth century. It was assumed that adults had an obligation to implant within children a sense of social responsibility, that is, to help prepare them for adult life. Interactions with children were not as haphazard as they had been in the past, and methods used and goals to be achieved in conditioning children were stressed.

Attitudes towards education changed. The prevailing attitude had been that all members of society be educated, whereas the new idea was that only the rich should be educated. The thought was that if the poor were educated they would not want to do the manual labor required in the growing technology. Education for all would destroy society. The result was a two-class system of education—one for the lower classes and another for the middle and upper classes. The idea of adapting a child's studies to his future trade or profession was spreading, and the children comprising the future manual labor pool were educated accordingly. Isolation was now complete. Children were separated from adults and from children of other classes.

The concept of a private life within the family, first seen in the seventeenth century, was now more fully developed. The fishbowl existence was becoming unknown. The old way emphasized how to live together communally, whereas the new way emphasized a respect for privacy. Nicknames were used in the confines of the family setting suggesting the need to separate the family from the rest of society. Health and education became the prime interests and duties of parents, lest their children humiliate them with unacceptable behavior.

Ideas of family life between the eighteenth century and our own have not changed significantly. Noteworthy though, was the recognition of adolescence as a distinct state of development. During the nineteenth century adolescence was the time for young men to be conscripted into the military; it was a proud time as they were no longer considered children. There is perhaps the subtle notion beginning here that even though childhood was an accepted stage of growth and development, the goal was to get through it and get on to the really important task of being an adult. This idea of future orientation is still with us.

So, by the nineteenth century, children were viewed as potential adults living in a society which needed well-behaved and contributing members. The ways in which these potential adults would be allowed to contribute were defined primarily by their social/economic status at birth. Through the educational process children were isolated from other adults by virtue of their age and class. The family as a unit grew in importance, and between the home and the school it was hoped that morals could be imparted and children molded into functional social beings.

CHILDREN: EDUCATED

With Charles Darwin's publications at the end of the nineteenth century, the child study movement began to flourish. This was partly the result of Darwin's suggestion that intelligence is determined by heredity. The concept of survival of the fittest, especially the question of why some humans seem to be more fit intellectually, took on prime importance. Darwin's work was subject to much debate and controversy, but for purposes of this discussion it is necessary to recognize the importance of his ideas and their impact on the formal study of children.

The first psychological laboratory was founded by Wilhelm Wundt in Germany in 1879. Psychology was in its infancy, and it is this date that marks for many its acceptance as a legitimate science. Wundt and his colleagues were primarily concerned with man's conscious experience; that is, they wanted to understand sensations, thoughts, and emotions. Their work was directed towards trying to answer some of the age-old questions about man's nature and behavior. Although the impact of their work was acknowledged in America, the emphasis in America was more on understanding objective behavior than conscious experience. In other words, American psychologists were more concerned with what people actually did than with what they felt. It was not until the past decade that the areas of feelings and emotions truly became accepted areas of study and concern.

Earlier American psychologists were strongly influenced by the works of Pavlov and of Watson. Mention of their ideas is important. Both men, and later their followers, viewed the human organism as a recipient; behavior was to be understood in terms of what was done to the organism. The view of the infant as an active and goal-seeking organism is a model which has been only recently recognized.

Ivan Petrovich Pavlov (Russian, 1849-1936) found from his study of animals that there are two sources of higher nervous activity. The first is the unconditioned reflex system, which governs innate reaction patterns to certain stimuli—for example, salivation at the sight of food. The second source is the sensory conditioning system, or first signaling system. This enables the organism to adapt to changes in its environment. Thus, for example, many animals learn through conditioning to react by fleeing when they merely see tracks or pick up scents of predatory animals. This process binds or ties the original unconditioned reflex to particular environmental cues that are necessary for survival. Man, according to Pavlov, possesses both these systems, but in addition has a second signaling system, governed by language, which allows for thought processes to function before he takes action. Language also makes it possible to generalize from one experience to another. This approach to understanding behavior views man as a passive organism. Things continually happen to him and individual instigation is minimal.

John B. Watson (American, 1878-1958) felt that behavior is real and objective and practical, while consciousness is a facet of fantasy; hence, he was labeled a Behaviorist and his school of psychology, Behaviorism. He asserted that behavior is nothing more than a series of conditioned reflexes—a set of responses learned by the process of classical conditioning. He taught that man was not born with any particular mental traits, abilities, or predispositions. All we inherit are a few inborn reflexes and all differences in behavior among people are merely the result of different learned responses. Also, whatever could be learned could be unlearned and there was no limit to what an individual might become if properly conditioned. Watson is said to have made the statement that he could take any infant and through proper conditioning make that child anything he (Watson) wanted him to be.

Watson's Behaviorism had an important influence on child-rearing practices during the 1920s and 1930s. Textbooks published on early childhood education prior to World War II reflect behaviorist theories with respect to habit training, socialization processes, and the lack of affect or concern with feelings in adult-child relationships. Parents were encouraged to keep infants on a strict schedule. Come hell or high water, the baby was to be bathed at a given time, put to bed at a given time, and receive a feeding at a given time.

My mother, for instance, used to tap the soles of my older brother's feet to wake him up for that 2 am feeding. These parents of my mother's generation only wanted to do what was right for their children; they did not, for the most part, feel confident to question or to challenge what the experts were saying. However, suffice it to say that by the time my mother's fifth child was born, he ate when he was hungry and behaviorism was ignored!

As influential as the behaviorist approach was, other theories were circulating. Psychologist Arnold Gesell, who first published in 1912, rejected the behaviorists' theories which he felt were stifling to the development of the young child. Gesell was convinced that the first six years of a child's life are his/her most important and that not only is the young child affected by the environment, but in turn strives to act upon the environment. Gesell's ideas are closer in theory to recent thinking supported by research.

The term "progressive education" antagonizes many people. This is unfortunate as many of its proponents' ideas have been misinterpreted and misapplied. John Dewey (American, 1859-1952) felt that the emphasis in education should be removed from the doings of the past and concentrated on the present in preparation for the future. Any material which is presented in the classroom must be related to the student's existence through his/her experiences. For example, all pupils must arrive at school somehow; if they arrive by bus, this could be a starting point for studies in communication, motor and engine mechanics, social manners, and the like, depending upon the age and interest of the students. These concepts can be used for future recall and judgmental processes because they were learned in an individually meaningful way.

The teacher must be cognizant of the socio-economic backgrounds of the students if he/she is to relate learnings to things with which the pupils are familiar. Self-discipline is a goal achieved through participation in and comprehension of the rules and ways of society, and a respect for the rights of one's neighbors; that is, everyone must be allowed to function as an individual within certain social limitations.

Dewey's ideas were picked up by many, perhaps in reaction to the rigidity and inflexibility of behaviorism, and translated into action, sometimes incorrectly and with dire consequences. In many cases people focused on "everyone must be allowed to function as an individual..." without regard for "...within certain social limitations." Individual freedom became synonymous with chaos in many settings and many adult-child relationships floundered and became unworkable. Many parents who wanted to be progressive but did not know how to implement Dewey's ideas lived with selfish and unmanageable children. It seems that even today many people equate Dewey's progressive education with blatant permissiveness. It is regrettable that the strengths of Dewey's thinking were not appreciated by many, but it is fortunate that a different approach to interacting with children was considered.

Another tributary feeding into the mainstream of ideas about childhood was founded by and named after Maria Montessori (Italian, 1870-1952). It might strike the reader that the Montessori Method, which is a well-publicized contemporary approach, is being incorrectly presented in a chronological sense. Actually, Montessori schools first appeared in this country in the early 1900s; then they closed almost as quickly as they had appeared. It has been only within the past fifteen years that the Montessori school has taken root and established itself as a bona fide member of respected early childhood models .

By 1916 there were about 200 authorized Montessori schools in this country and another 2,000 or so using her name and methods. In 1914 William H. Kilpatrick, an influential writer and personal friend of John Dewey's, published *The Montessori Method*

Examined, which brought an end to the Montessori schools in this country for over thirty years. Kilpatrick, who was a devout follower of Dewey at the time, criticized the Montessori approach as being too restrictive of children's individuality; he suggested that the intensive practice of skills could not be generalized to other areas of experience.

The Montessori Method is based upon a prepared environment, an organized and coordinated set of materials and equipment. The materials are designed for sequential use and are to be used in definite well-defined ways. The children are not encouraged to do their own thing with the materials. By living in this prepared environment the children are given skills in motor, sensory, and language education. In short, the Montessori approach emphasizes a natural process of education in which the learner acts upon the environment. The role of the adult is to prepare the environment and to act as a resource person, a catalyst for the child as he/she grows and develops.

During World War II many mothers who had previously been at-home were recruited into the labor force to replace men on active duty. Federal funds were allocated and all types of day care centers were set up while mothers worked. (Federal funds were suspended a few months after the end of the war.) These day care centers were, for the most part, staffed by well-qualified people who were capable of studying children in these environments.

Coupled with this was the growing influence of psychoanalytic theory with its emphasis on early childhood experiences. Research abounded. By 1946 Benjamin Spock had published his first baby and child guide which advocated that children be allowed to learn in their own way and at their own pace. In 1950 Erik Erikson published his first edition of *Childhood and Society* which dealt with the concept of a healthy personality for every child. The groundwork was being laid for the explosion of new ideas and changing conceptions about the nature of man and the potential of the child.

The 1960s was an exciting decade with early childhood research appearing at a previously unparalleled rate. This research has brought new insights in such areas of growth and development as the nature of psychological development during infancy; human motivation; cognitive and affective development; acquisition of language; and effects of early stimulation. The notion that intelligence is fixed or is genetically predetermined has been challenged. It is now inferred that intelligence is an active on-going process of development at its highest point of acceleration during the first five years of a child's life. It is recognized that from the moment of birth (perhaps conception) the human organism is active and goal-seeking. This implies that children do not thrive when the environment merely acts upon them. It seems that by nature infants and children strive to adapt to and manipulate the environment.

These new assumptions about childhood growth and development ran contrary to many previous ideas. We are probably just at the start of a scientific understanding of the human organism. In view of new research and new ideas, we feel more comfortable in considering different ways of interacting with children. Some of our traditional approaches to child-rearing result from the limited information available at earlier times. Our present ways of viewing children and childhood are grounded in modes of thought and theories and philosophies that many of us have never really questioned. Recognizing that attitudes and conceptions about children have undergone significant and discernible changes through the centuries is perhaps the first step towards a questioning and re-evaluation process. A new concern for children and specifically children's rights may be just on the horizon partly as a result of the feminist movement. The feminist movement and the Civil Rights activities of the 1960s no doubt have helped pave the way for thinking about children in this context.

Some of the writers who have recently dealt with interacting with children in more humanistic ways include John Holt, Herbert Kohl, Haim Ginott, and James Herndon. These writers have published books which have reached beyond professional readers.

My own thinking is concerned with some possible "Why's— why we in fact cling to many of our present attitudes about childhood—and some "How's"—how to lessen the abyss between ideas and action. If we do not facilitate this transition, new ideas remain in a vacuum to be rejected, discarded, or even openly scoffed at. Richard Farson is a psychologist concerned with present child-rearing practices. Following are some excerpts from his recent book *Birthrights*. The reader is not asked to agree or disagree with them; the issue is whether it is fair or acceptable to treat the man as some kind of a "kook."

> The ideal child is cute (entertaining to adults), well-behaved (doesn't bother adults), and bright (capable of bringing home report cards the parents can be proud of).

In fact, never before in history have parents and teachers had so much 'understanding' of children, or at least of their physical and social development. But the understanding has not led to improved conditions for children, but simply more control of them and consequently more burdensome responsibilities of supervision for parents.

The degrees of oppression vary, but one kind is universal; that children have no alternative but to live with their parents or be housed by the government in some jail-like alternative.

It is interesting to note that in a recent interview the interviewer made the comment "Yeah but, children need..." and allowed Farson to respond only after he (the interviewer) had attempted to put Farson down by making a joke of one of his ideas. Serious recipients of new ideas should have nothing to lose by hearing out a different idea. The new idea can do only one of two things: either reinforce a previously held attitude or belief, or open new vistas for new thinking. Fear or panic reactions stagnate us and make further personal growth impossible. Serious writers should be received with interest, not as sources of threat, and certainly not as sources of ridicule.

Roger W. McIntire, a professor at the University of Maryland, is a proponent of a mandatory licensing program for parents, or mandatory birth control. McIntire says: "Why should the government have a say in whether I have a child? Because the last century has shown that the government will be saddled with most of the burden of raising your child (McIntire, p. 132)." Further, he suggests that there is some type of absurd reasoning functioning that requires an education and a license to drive a car, but allows anybody to "raise our most precious possession or to add to the burden of this possession without demonstrating an ability to parent (p. 39)."

The topics suggested for such a licensing program include: principles of sound nutrition and diet; understanding changes in nutritional requirements with age; principles of general hygiene and health; principles of behavioral development; principles of learning and language acquisition; and principles of modeling, imitation, reinforcement, and punishment. McIntire suggests that such a program might be offered as an alternative to jail for child-abuse offenders; I would suggest that such a program might be instituted as a required part of the high school curriculum. Regardless of the acceptance or rejection of such an idea, it is presented as an example of recent concern for children.

Another approach to modifying attitudes about children is the "Free To Be...You And Me" series sponsored by *Ms. Magazine*. What is particularly interesting about this program is that it almost by-passes adults completely and attempts to deal directly with attitudes children have about themselves. A "Story For Free Children" appears in each issue, and related record albums are available. A "Free To Be...You And Me" television program was viewed by adults and children all over the country. Apparently this program was so well received that we can look forward to similar programs in the future. The primary thrust of the series is to break down male and female stereotypes which limit children's options. This is an important step in allowing children full range in personal growth and development and it is indicative of another emerging area with regard to changing ideas and attitudes about children. We may not ultimately accept these new ideas, but it is imperative that we try to understand them.

Chapter 1 has set the stage by considering the concept of childhood and ideas and attitudes about the nature of children in terms of a historical perspective. This chronological description helps explain the derivation of present ideas and attitudes. It is apparent that many of the approaches we use in interacting with children are grounded in institutions and mores which are not in concert with more recent scientific findings about children. It is difficult to reconcile the old with the new as long as so many of us vigorously defend that which we have never questioned. Therefore, it is time to question and to re-evaluate, and that is what the remainder of this book will attempt to do.

2

*"I can't believe you just sit there and do nothing
while those children squabble."*

*"Well, I want to give them a chance to settle their
own differences without my interfering."*

"Yeah but, children need

Authority

AND SO THEY DO. Children even allocate authority to adults, especially their own parents. As Thomas Gordon, clinical psychologist and founder of Parent/Teacher Effectiveness Training, points out,

> To the young child there seems nothing his parents do not know, nothing they cannot do. He marvels at the breadth of their understanding, the accuracy of their predictions, the wisdom of their judgment (p. 166).

So much for the topic of authority. Adults agree that children need it and children's behavior suggests that they want it. At first glance this seems adequate and sensible, but anyone who has interacted with children recognizes that something is amiss with the simplicity of this explanation. How do we account for the constant clashes and conflicts between the authority figure and the recipients of the authority?

I have had informal discussions about the concept of authority with educators, parents, military personnel, and scientists. Inevitably these discussions have centered on diverse "Yeah buttings..."; it became very apparent that people were approaching the discussions from different perspectives. We always agreed that authority was needed but from that point on opinions branched off in many directions. The points of dissension involved the process, or the How's, of implementing authority.

The problem crystallized for me recently. I concluded that what might be at issue was a simple definition problem, so I turned to the dictionary. According to *The Random House Dictionary*, authority is "the power to determine, adjudicate, or otherwise settle issues or disputes; jurisdiction; the right to control, command, or determine." This definition did not exactly coincide with my own concept of authority, so I read on... "A power or right delegated or given; an accepted source of information, advice. Synonyms; Control, Influence." And it was at this point that I was clouted by the "Ah-ha phenomenon." Some people use their authority to control; other use it to influence. Some people assume or take authority; others use it when it is delegated or given to them. This is the key to understanding authority and what it means to different people.

Traditionally authority has meant controlling, whereas more recently, people have started using it to influence. People probably do not use their authority in these two ways interchangeably. We are either control-oriented or influence-oriented. We seldom think about how and why we tend to use our authority. There are, however, reasons why we favor one orientation over the other. Both have to be discussed.

AUTHORITY BY CONTROL

In my elementary school teaching days I started every school year the same way. I all but put on Gestapo boots and a leather coat as I faced the class. If it meant tossing someone out in the hall that first day, that was okay; the kids were going to know that I was not someone to be trifled with. I was tough and the children had better watch their step! They could count on a most unpleasant experience if they dared break one of my rules. But by June we would cry together as we read *Charlotte's Web*, howl with laughter over *Homer Price*, and on the last day of school I could be counted on to be a sobbing heap as I kissed each student farewell. (One boy refused my bon voyage embrace in front of the class, but he did sneak back later to collect it.)

That was June. But what was happening in September? I did not trust the children to respond to me unless they were first afraid of me. From fear and intimidation would evolve mutual respect and genuine caring. The reader might be thinking at this point, "Well, it worked, didn't it?" No, it did not. Nothing ever began to happen in my classrooms until I had finally relinquished my fear tactics. I was playing a role and a very time-consuming one.

Behind the terror in their eyes were some incredibly good children, but I had created a situation that did not allow any of that goodness to come through. The children were too busy trying not to cross me and I was too busy making sure they didn't. I was convinced that if they were not terror-stricken at the outset they could not accept the "real me" who tends to be an informal and flexible type of person.

In effect, I was implying that the children were not entitled to know me until they had first proven to me they were worthy of knowing me. This being worthy of me was defined in terms of how much trembling they did when I spoke. I convinced myself that I was establishing respect, but what I was really establishing was my own need to be their undisputed leader. The irony was that there never was any question at the outset as to who was the authority in that classroom. I already had my position of leadership but I felt it necessary to go through a ritual of instilling fear because I did not trust the students or myself.

I thought the students were out to test me and to try to make me look foolish and incompetent. Well, I would show them! And I did. I showed them that they were right, but it was by my own engineering! In short, every September for five years I showed a group of youngsters that an adult who does not trust children is more than capable of eliciting fear from them. My only consolation is my memories of the Junes of those years.

This is one of the underlying assumptions of authority by control—that is, that children cannot be trusted to behave in acceptable and responsible ways unless someone is around to make sure that they do. The tools used to implement this are fear and intimidation. However, as children get older, this use of fear becomes less effective in many home and school settings. Gordon suggests that

> Using power to control children works only under special conditions. The parent must be sure to *possess the power*-....But a person has power over another only as long as the second is in a position of weakness, want, need, deprivation, helplessness, dependency (p. 170).

As children mature, many challenge this use of power and control as they develop the confidence and the resources to meet their own needs. Parents and adults often continue to use methods of authority that were effective when the children were younger, more dependent, and more fearful, only to find that these same

subject would always be the teacher; the pseudo-respondent was always the learner.

The experimenter explained the task. The learner was to be taught a list of word associations which would be read to him by the teacher. Also, it was explained, the teacher would give the learner an electric shock through electrodes each time the learner made a mistake. The shocks were described as being painful but not capable of causing permanent damage. The teacher was seated before an apparatus containing thirty switches labeled "15 volts" up to "450 volts" in 15-volt increments. The switches were grouped and labeled from "slight shock" up to "danger—severe shock!" The teacher was instructed to increase the intensity of the shock every time the learner made a mistake. The teacher was not administering real shocks, but he had no way of knowing this . The learner followed a predetermined script of responses, including appropriate moans and groans when he was supposedly being shocked.

The most significant result of the study was that a large proportion of the teachers proceeded right up through the graduated range of shocks even when the learner was screaming "in pain" for the experiment to stop. If the teacher seemed ready to stop the experiment the experimenter would sternly encourage the teacher to continue. "You must go on. You have no other choice." Some of the teachers did refuse to continue, but many proceeded at the experimenter's command. Some of the teachers blamed the learner for being stupid. Sixty-five percent of the teachers gave shocks right up to the top of the shock range.

A group of psychiatrists had estimated .1 percent obedience or that slightly more than one person in a thousand would go right up the shock range. They described the ones who would administer the high-voltage shocks as lunatics and psychopaths. To repeat, Milgram found 65 percent obedience. In discussing the results of this study R. J. Herrnstein (1974) suggests that the data

...show us, not precisely that people are callous, but that they can slip into a frame of mind in which their actions are not entirely their own. Psychologically, it is not they alone who are flipping the switches, but also the institutional authority—the austere scientist in the laboratory coat. The authority is taken to have the right to do what he is doing, by virtue of knowledge and/or status (p. 85).

All persons who reacted to the experiment emphasized in no uncertain terms that they know they personally would not have continued with the administration of the shocks. (The simplicity of retrospect!) However, it is pointed out that the hundreds of participants in the actual experiment represented a genuine cross-section of the population.

Is there any correlation between the studies cited and a power authority saying to a child, "You will eat your spinach or else"? Ingrained attitudes towards authority take root over a period of time. The fear of what will happen if the green leafy stuff is not eaten and the fear of not administering those shocks are all a part of an attitudinal dimension. Herrnstein (1974) suggests that the subjects in the Milgram study

> ... simply did not apply the usual standards of humanity to their own conduct. Or, rather, the usual standards gave way to a more pressing imperative, the command of authority (p. 85).

Further, "Ordinary people, will in fact, not easily engage in brutality on their own. But they will apparently do so if someone else is in charge (Herrnstein, p. 85)." Some people think that control and power types of authority are potentially and ultimately capable of producing unquestioned acceptance of authority while at the same time assuming that responsible and inner-directed behavior will at another time result. This assumption seems fallacious upon scrutiny.

In addition to the recipient of power and control being externally influenced, it is suggested that the authority figure exerting the control is in turn externally influenced. That is, authorities who depend upon power seem to be concerned with the "How do I look in the eyes of others?" phenomenon. In my elementary teaching days this was of paramount concern for me. I needed my principal's comments such as "Gee, Karen. No doubt about it. You've got those kids under your thumb," or, "That Karen sure runs a tight ship. Those kids know better than to breathe out of turn in her room." So I would march my class down the hall confident that my wrath prevented them from chatting or missing a step in line. With head held high and chin jutting forward I felt that I had the esteem and respect of all my colleagues.

Later in the year when I was able to abandon the power role, I could casually remind the kids that if we cut up in the halls it tended to disturb other classrooms and that I would appreciate not having to be chewed out by anyone for noise. We would laugh, someone would do an imitation of the principal (accurately!), I would pretend I didn't see it, and off we would go, quietly. Under these circumstances it was not fear that prevented them from making noise but rather a response to the comradery and rapport we had developed in the absence of tyranny. They were responding to my request as Karen The Person and I did not have a need to bark at them so my colleagues would nod approvingly. Hoping my peers thought I was a tremendous teacher did not matter. What mattered was my relationship with the children in the classroom.

I do not think my concern with how my peers might be evaluating me is an isolated experience. I observe too many adults really putting children down, really coming on strong with the power and control, turning to other adults around them and saying something like, "Ho. Ho. You really have to stay on top of these kids these days." It is almost a plea for confirmation. Usually the other adult will agree how unruly and difficult kids are today. This supposedly justifies the grueling and demeaning treatment the children have just undergone.

The supreme compliment for many adults is to be told by another adult that he/she really knows how to handle kids—not *interact* with children, but *handle* them. The need for external approval and justification for using power to control children is rarely questioned. It is not easy to ask oneself the question, "Why do I really feel a need to control children?" It is easier to rationalize the answer with such thoughts as: "Because I am responsible for raising my children"; "I have an obligation to teach them social expectations"; "It is my duty to raise well-behaved, contributing and productive citizens." Such intentions, that is, rationalizations, are above questioning. What requires thought and consideration is HOW many of us blindly and unquestioningly try to make our intentions and goals realities.

After many years of questioning, delving, and re-evaluating, I have been able to answer for myself the question of why I felt a need to control children. Very simply, I was afraid that if I interacted with children without the guise of control and power the children would not accept me. This fear that children would not respond to me on a person-to-person level necessitated my instilling fear in them. In return I gained obedience from the children and a feeling of respect from my colleagues, both very worthy of my efforts, or so I thought.

In reality, I sacrificed numerous opportunities for the children to develop inner self-directed behavior and I reinforced a prevalent feeling among them that they were unworthy of trust from adults. That supposed respect from my peers was a game within a game, in that most of them were also into the power and control approach. It became a matter of which of us could wield the greatest amount of control over our children and which of us could make more children fearful.

In short, I personally felt a need to control children because I dreaded being rejected if I interacted with them solely on the basis of what I, a vulnerable and sensitive person, had to offer. I went to great lengths to make sure that I appeared invulnerable and infallible in the children's eyes. They could never know that it would hurt me tremendously if I allowed them to see me as I really was—vulnerable.

I averted this possibility by asserting power and control and by convincing myself that it really didn't matter whether or not they liked me. I had a job to do and that was all that counted. I even found myself entertaining rationalizations such as: "They will thank me when they get older for my being tough now"; "I only treat them this way because I care about them"; "They'll understand why I treated them this way when they grow up and are parents and teachers."

Such rationalizations obviously reek of guilt, another re-affirmation of a lack of trust in children. The underlying meassage is "You are too young and inexperienced to appreciate what I am doing," but inserting different adjectives does not alter the true message that "You are too dumb and stupid to know that this is good for you." I question how good something is if we invest incredible amounts of time and energy in convincing its recipients of our goodness! When we feel guilty about something we are doing and make apologizing remarks to defend our behavior, it is time to scrutinize what we are defending.

Why do so many of us feel a need to control the thoughts, actions, and behaviors of children? As it turns out, we can control isolated bits of children's overt behavior, but we can never control their internal thoughts. Usually we aren't interested in children's reactions to our treatment of them. To allow their thoughts and feelings to be verbalized would force us to deal with our needs to control them and because this is so anxiety-provoking it is avoided. "You are always telling me what to do," or "I never get to do what I want to do" or any of the other awkward and clumsy statements children are apt to make are a source of great threat for many adults.

Children are usually answered at these times with the standard "It is for your own good" rationalizations. Some children are banished from the adult's company under the guise of lacking respect for elders and being sassy. "I will not tolerate such disrespectful, insolent and impertinent behavior" is usually a righteous kind of cover-up for "I really don't know why I push you around and I am afraid to find out." It seems apparent that children are not accepting such adult diversionary tactics or we would not have the many conflicts that we do have with children.

This is not to suggest that conflicts are avoidable, or for that matter, even undesirable. Conflicts make intra- and inter-personal growth possible. A clash of needs creates a situation in which the participants can examine what they need, why they feel they need it, and how they might realize or satisfy their needs while at the same time recognizing that another person is involved in the same process. Many conflicts which arise out of individual striving can be a healthy and necessary source of growth.

However, in an adult-child conflict, the needs of the child usually become secondary or even subservient to the needs of the adult. The resolution of conflict is often mandated by decree and in effect the child is told that his/her needs are not valid, or at least not as valid as the needs of the adult.

Say a child wants to stay up to watch a special television program; the parent however, wants and needs some time alone. The child, usually after a fracas of some kind, is exiled to the bedroom at the usual bedtime accompanied by the "You need your sleep" and "I am your parent" and "I care about you..." routine. The child is indirectly told that his/her wanting to see the program was a dumb idea. What the parent wants takes priority over what the child wants. The parent often disguises the true meaning behind such a decision. Rather than being honest about a need to be alone, a need to be away from the child, he/she gives the child another dose of "This is for your own good." This situation could result in two people working through a need conflict, but all too often it brings out the same old authority by control.

Then there are those conflicts which adults anticipate, look for, and plan for, i.e., the terrible two's and the rebellious teens. These stages of growth and development are treated as if every male and female has innate genes that erupt into action—one at age two or so, and the other around thirteen. The terrible two's and the rebellious teens are, for the most part, adult-created myths. Granted, these are difficult times for children, but it seems that adults complicate these ages further. Around age two a child is developing a sense of Me, a sense of separateness from the people and objects in the environment. The child tries to assert his/her Me-ness—"Mine, I want..., No, Give me." Parents tend to react to these attempts at growth and individualization by trying to show the child who the boss is. The child *knows* who the boss is; that is not what is at issue. The child is trying to structure reality, make sense of the environment, and find his/her place in it.

The two-year-old needs help in defining many of his/her needs and in being made aware of others' needs; one of his/her primary needs does not include the establishment of authority. The child already has this sense of authority and is aware of it. So the typical "NO!" response of the two-year-old is not a premeditated act of defiance. It is not an example of the young trying to usurp the power of the older. It is in fact a plea for a partnership in development and a demand to be recognized and guided.

Meanwhile, many adults are so afraid of raising an unmanageable monster that they come crashing down with all the power and control they can muster. The parents usually have an eye to the future, probably anticipating the rebellious teens, and often become obsessed with showing the child who runs the show. The child finds himself/herself repeatedly thwarted by controlling parents as he/she pursues the inevitable chores of being a two-year-old. The trusting threes, I suspect, is a time of rejuvenation after feeling beaten down and submissive from the preceding year.

The rebellious teens gene is said to erupt somewhere around age 13 and to be in a state of continuous activity for about five or six years. These are difficult years for young people when one considers all the physical and psychological changes involved. Parents complain that they can't control their children anymore. This is correct—they can't. As mentioned previously, control works or is effective only as long as the recipient of the control is in a state of weakness and dependency. Young teens are becoming aware of their own strengths, resources, and successes at being autonomous. The last thing they want or need is to be controlled.

Meanwhile, parents sense and observe changes in their children as they become or try to become more independent, and, out of fear of losing control, many adults try to assert more control. Their fear is well-grounded. By the teen years they have lost control because they no longer possess the power in the eyes of their children that they had when the children were younger. The children gradually join the major league while the adults are still trying to play by minor league rules. It is difficult for parents to realize that their children no longer accept them as managers. Parents find themselves warming the bench and they fight like hell to get back to managing. The harder they try, the more insistent their children become on keeping them on the bench.

Parents tend to feel that their children are rejecting them, but it seems more accurate to say teenagers are rebelling against adults' attempts at exerting more control and power over them, not against adults *per se*. In short, it is suggested that adult-child conflicts are intensified and complicated in situations in which adults attempt to use power and control approaches in resolving them. The time period is increased, further, often over a period of years, because the children's needs in such conflicts are rarely dealt with.

Contemporary consumer magazines often publish articles related to child-rearing practices. Such publications are read by millions of parents and educators and their points of view have a wide influence. In the *Reader's Guide to Periodical Literature* under the heading "Children," amazingly enough, articles on child-rearing can be found under the sub-heading called "Management and Training." It is hard to believe that the listed articles deal with people and not with lower forms of life. To find articles about interacting with children under such a sub-heading is truly vexing and surprising!   But at least a few of the listed articles dealt with control and power approaches to authority. One recent one states:

> On the contrary, as we adults have surrendered more and more of our once unquestioned leadership, substituting appeasement for authority, our children have become not liberated, but confused (Eliasberg, p. 40).

Eliasberg seems to suggest that it is an evil practice for children and adults to question leadership. There seems to be a yearning for the good old days when our methods of dealing with children were merely accepted. There is a subtle pressure here that opposes a questioning process.

The implication seems to be that if certain people had not tampered with the status quo, we would not have all the problems with children that we do. If I were a reader searching for expertise in the area of child-rearing I would be apt to conclude that "boat-rocking" is taboo and that I had better plod on with more traditional practices. I would have to conclude that any problems I might be having with children were resulting from my being inept at implementing established practices, not that it might be worthwhile for me to question them. Eliasberg implies that if one does choose to "surrender more and more of our once unquestioned leadership," the only replacement for such control is appeasement, i.e., abandon your control and power and you will have to rely on soothing, placating, and assuaging children. And, after they have been soothed, placated, and assuaged, they ultimately will be confused.

As a reader, so am I! Adults do not like to be appeased and there is no reason to believe that children thrive on such artificial treatment, either. The writer of the article obviously has no intention of questioning the underlying implications of the authority concept to which she alludes, and it is probable that most readers are likewise deterred.

In another article, originally a speech on "Eroding Authority," U.S. Supreme Court Justice Lewis F. Powell, Jr. (1972) discusses how the character of people in the past was shaped by "humanizing authority," and how today we find ourselves cut adrift from this. He then points out how old values and ethics are threatened by new ones and how this process is the result of changes beyond our control, such as advances in science and technology, urbanization, and mass transportation and communication. Powell sees this as a time of "unanchored individualization," that is, a time to do your own thing. Further, "It has become increasingly fashionable to question and attack the most basic elements in our society (p. 753)," and as a result we have lost sight of the importance of historical perspective.

Lastly, Powell lists those values he holds, including a sense of honor, duty, loyalty, self-discipline, and patriotism. At no time does the writer actually discuss the relationship between eroding authority and different values emerging today. It seems that anyone who questions authority and/or values is to be accused of trying to be fashionable, which makes the effort seem frivolous. Such frivolity obviously leads to an erosion of values. The reader is once more subtly pressured into accepting the status quo. "Do not question, as at best it is an idle and trivial pastime."

Authority which is grounded in control and power then, suggests that adults are unable to trust children. In other words, they cannot trust children to respond in positive and meaningful ways unless the children are first afraid and fearful of adults. It is as if there were a cold war going on between children and adults. Adults who do not trust children are in effect saying that children are "out to get" them, to degrade them, to make them appear incompetent and ineffectual. This war is designed by adults, and kids are forced to participate in it in defensive and at times untrustworthy ways.

Adults look at the behavior of children, which by necessity is often defensive because they are not trusted to behave any other way, and they conclude that children are by nature devious and undeserving of our trust. Many adults tend to treat children as causes of this lack of trust, when in reality children are merely reacting to a lack of trust on the part of adults. Further, this lack of trust says that children do not want to, and *will not,* behave in acceptable and responsible ways unless some adult is hovering over them to make sure that they do. This requires constant nagging and prodding and many children cannot be trusted to continue the desired behavior in the absence of control and power. Such situations exist, but not because children are inherently irresponsible; rather, children will resort to other forms of behavior in the absence of external pressure because the reasons why their needs are not being met were not considered. The control factor does not really help a child change internally, only externally.

Another implication of authority by control is that after the ground-work has been laid by forcing children to behave in certain ways, they will be responsible and inner-directed when they get older. There is research to suggest that children who learn early to depend upon external control extend this dependency into their adult years. The lesson is often too well learned. Many children do become convinced that they are incapable of functioning in the absence of power and control figures, and as adults they continue to seek external constraints and definitions of what they should be doing. Their lives take on meaning and direction only through the eyes of others. Obedience then can become equated with self-esteem and acceptance.

Adults who rely on asserting their authority through control and power need to answer the question: "Why do I feel a need to control someone else's behavior?" The common rationalizations sometimes used in answering this question have been discussed, but falling back on rationalizations is not the same as meeting the question head on. It has been suggested that control and power figures are very concerned with how they look in the eyes of their peers. They are apt to ask themselves such questions as: "Am I coming across as someone who is strong?" "Do I look as if I really have these kids under control?" "What will I do if some child makes me look bad in front of another adult?"

Lastly, authority by control and power involves guilt. Why else would adults feel compelled to assure children that in spite of appearances, what they are doing is really for the children's own good? Should not something that is good be self-evident? Do we really have to sell goodness? After all is said and done, many adults need to answer this question: Why do I feel a need to control children's behavior?

AUTHORITY BY INFLUENCE

The key to understanding and appreciating authority by influence centers around *trust*. In effect the adult strives to convey to the child that he/she is trusted and that nothing is more important than the relationship which exists between them. One does not foist his/her knowledge on a child until that child expresses a need or desire to learn what can be offered.

This is what authority by influence is all about. As adults we recognize that we have acquired many skills, experiences, ideas, and concepts which have enriched our lives and/or have enabled us to meet the responsibilities of everyday living. Authority by control attempts to impose this knowledge on a child whereas authority by influence attempts to put across ideas through persuasion and inducement. A climate is created in which the child knows that the adult cares about him/her and will act in an advisory capacity *when invited to do so.*

To act as what Gordon (1970) calls a consultant requires an enormous amount of restraint on the part of the adult because so often we just "know" we have the data and information the child needs. By holding back and not unduly giving answers, solutions, and information, we are giving a child this message: "I have this unbounded faith in you, but I want you to know that I am here on the sidelines ready and willing to pitch in if you need and want my help."

This approach involves a risk on the part of adults since self-esteems can plummet and egos can be deflated when it becomes apparent that many children do not think enough of certain adults to seek out their advice and assistance. To prevent this situation from arising, some adults, as already implied, simply rely on authority by control. "You will do as I say or else," is easier to say than, "I have some experiences and ideas to share with you *if you are interested.*" In the latter case one risks being told by a child, "You just don't make it in my book as a person. I'll have to take it from you if you lord it over me, but if you give me a choice, I'd just as soon you'd buzz off."

It often proves difficult to hold back, restrain oneself, and not interfere in children's activities, especially their battles, unless the children themselves request some input. Time after time I have been tempted to assert *my* wisdom and knowledge as an adult in numerous squabbles (which are such an ingrained part of child-to-child interactions). I want to jump into the middle of things with my "Bobby, you take the mini-bike and Lee, you take the wagon," following up with verbalizations on the didactics of sharing. I watch kids struggle and I want to make things perfect in the shortest time possible!

But holding back pays off. Kids prove themselves perfectly capable of reaching their own solutions without an outsider trying to run things; I am forever amazed at the solutions they come up with—often more effective than the solutions adults might have come up with. In my own case, after some years children have learned that I will not take on their problems for them; so I am no longer harassed with them coming to me to complain about how so-and-so is treating them, etc.

This is not to suggest that I sit back reveling in my ability to use self-restraint as one child beats another to a bloody pulp before my eyes. I can make it very clear that certain behavior is totally unacceptable and why, but then I have to resist the temptation to "handle" the situation with methods that I consider acceptable. Fading back out of children's clashes is difficult, but one can make a conscious effort to do so because of the rewards that come from authority by influence.

I have genuinely good feelings about my relationships with the neighborhood kids. They like me and trust me enough to share stories and thoughts with me that they do not wish to be shared with other adults. In the past they used to preface their tid-bits with "Now don't tell my mother." I have passed their test of trust and now they don't feel they have to remind me that they speak in confidence. This trust has taken a couple of years to develop. On a few occasions I have let something confidential slip in front of the wrong person and I have had to grovel at some child's feet in apology. I add that the embarrassment I have felt at those times is identical to that I have felt in similar situations with adults. Many times a kid approaches me with, "Hey Karen, I've got this problem..." and I am overwhelmed with feelings of joy and pride—some child thinks enough of me to seek me out.

I work at using authority by influence because it has not been easy for me to relinquish my authority by control. It is one thing to say "Yeah, this is how I really want to be" and quite another thing to actually be that person. Change does not come readily, but fortunately I have been able to learn workable and realistic skills. I personally have not completely integrated authority by influence into my being, nor have I completely abandoned authority by control, but I have gained tremendous support from friends and acquaintances involved in the same transitional process.

In relationships that I have developed with children I feel a great sense of relief that I don't have to concern myself with what I will do if they challenge my authority. There is nothing to challenge and I don't have to play the "what if?" game when I make requests of them. I have had them tell me that they don't feel like cleaning up the mess they have left in my living room, but I don't have to go through the "Well, you just won't be able to play here next time" routine.

I trust enough in our relationship to tell them that I really feel taken advantage of and that I don't appreciate being treated like a slave placed on earth for their convenience. This appeal, in essence based on our relationship and not on authority by control, is part of our mutual respect for working things through. It is reassuring when it is standard practice for the kids to straighten up after they've finished playing without my having to point out that our house is a shambles. I observe such development of responsible and inner-directed behavior and I know that the time and effort invested in trying to interact with children by using authority by influence is more than worthwhile.

As noted already, adults who rely on authority by control in interacting with children seem to be concerned with how they look in the eyes of their peers. Ideally, people using authority by influence would not care. Their only concern would be with developing a good relationship with children. It is difficult not to at least give some thought to how things might be interpreted by other adults. One theoretically shouldn't care, but nevertheless, one must be aware of the potential effects of this phenomenon.

Adults are quick to point out children's behaviors which they find unacceptable and would like to see changed, but very few children are encouraged or allowed to evaluate adults' behavior. A child I know is very aware that his mother and I are making great efforts to acknowledge the validity and importance of his needs and feelings. One day Linda and I were driving along with Ben (aged 7) in the back seat while we were gabbing on about something which did not include him in the conversation. All of a sudden Ben piped up from the rear, "I am not supposed to curse, so I don't think you two should use 'dirty talk' in front of me." Linda and I looked at each other with raised eyebrows. Having always considered our vocabularies colorful but certainly not offensive, we thanked Ben for sharing that with us. He can now be counted on to remind us if our language tends to get "out of line."

Of course this is probably a case of the youngster's testing us as he tries to define his role in his changing relationship with his mother and adults in general. Had we questioned the motivation telling him that what he said was trivial, immature, phony—in short, dumb. Linda and I talked about this later and it made us realize how we as adults want unquestioned acceptance from children and other adults, but how we tend to forget that children want the same from us.

Gordon (1970) discusses how at some time in the developing years some kids fire their parents. They make it very clear that their greatest wish is to get as far away as possible from their parents. The warning signs are given over a period of time prior to the actual firing and many adults have experienced them. Parents and other adults who bemoan the fact that children don't listen to them, don't respect them, and generally are in a state of conflict with them, are being given the message that their job is in jeopardy. It is more than likely that those parents who are fired have relied on authority by control.

Parents who use authority by influence really have nothing from which to be fired! If an adult has consistently shared information and experiences with children, then as the involved children assume more responsibility and maturity, the influence of the adult will be requested less and less and will eventually taper off. Nothing has really changed except the amount of influence. The adult-child relationship is intact, so one need not worry about being fired from a position never held. I have to agree with Gordon that many parents have let their relationships with their children disintegrate so much that their ultimate firing is inevitable.

But adults feel an obligation to teach their children social expectations and want to be assured that youngsters will mature into responsible and self-disciplined adults. Research on the modeling effect ("Practice what you preach"), bears out the validity of this maxim. Children not only directly imitate what they observe others around them doing, but they model behavior;

that is, they incorporate patterns of behavior into their repertoires and utilize and generalize them in situations long after the actual modeling process. Psychologist Albert Bandura's work (1970) further suggests that a child can observe how something is done and not practice the behavior at the time he/she observes it, but can use it long after anyone can even remember the original incident.

If we want responsible children, we adults must act in responsible ways. If we want self-initiated behavior in children, we ourselves must act in self-directed ways. One cannot develop inner-directed modes of behavior in children by always telling them what to do. If we want our children to be responsible for themselves and their actions, we must provide opportunities for this quality to develop. Authority by control stifles this behavior; authority by influence makes it possible.

Authority by control encourages an authority "hierarchy." Big people push kids around, kids model this behavior and push smaller kids around, and on down it goes until the smallest kid is squishing ants on the sidewalk!

Authority by influence offers different kinds of models so that children do not conclude that a benefit of age is having the right to tell other people what to do. Their influence models teach them that everyone, regardless of age, has something in terms of information and experiences to share. People become resources rather than sources of fear and intimidation.

But,

> The truth is, when parents are totally permissive, they're not giving the child freedom, they're depriving him of something he desperately needs—adult guidance and support. In comparison with the grownups who surround them, small children feel helpless. They need help in learning acceptable behavior, distinguishing right from wrong. They need to know how their parents *really* feel if they're to admit and express their own emotions. They also need help in controlling these emotions (Brothers, pp. 72-73).

The key words are guidance and support which are very different from control and imposition.

There is another potential threat for adults implementing authority by influence. Many adults just do not like to share feelings and emotions with other people, much less children. Sharing feelings often entails letting the other person know that what he/she has said or done hurts; to admit hurt is to admit vulnerability, and to admit vulnerability gives the other person a source of power—the power to affect or make an impact on someone. Many adults would not want a child to know that he/she possesses such power! Authority by control, on the other hand, does not have to deal so directly with feelings and emotions.

Many adults have either perpetrated or witnessed this typical dinner table scene: "You may not leave the table until you have eaten all your vegetables." Much hassling later, the child has either eaten the food, stuffed it in the drawer of the kitchen table, or actually vomited. It doesn't really matter which path is taken. The adult-child relationship has been chipped at. The child is bound to feel some hatred, hostility, and resentment toward the adult, and the adult, who really has the very best of intentions, has not affected the child's dietary habits except in a negative way. Many parents feel compelled to have authority over such matters as choice of foods, and with good reason. But

> In the absence of adult tyranny, adult judgment and information have to be the primary influence and are more likely to be accepted (Farson, p. 71).

According to Rita Kramer (1969) the child learns to rely on the parent for advice and protection. "He grows up respecting adult authority; he sees it as a source of protection when he needs it (p. 105)." She has categorized parents as generally falling into one of three groups: there is first, the controlling parent who does everything for the child—either to get things done or to spare the child frustration; second, there is the totally *laissez-faire* or permissive parent; and third, there is the parent who will let the child use his/her own resources, and will let him/her struggle. Parents of this third type act "as anchors. They have to maintain their principles without imposing them forcibly (p. 105)." It is an easy enough matter to categorize our friends who are parents, but perhaps we tend to become somewhat defensive when we attempt to classify ourselves. "Yeah but...!"

Authority by influence involves a great deal of risk. Adults who practice it have nothing to offer kids except themselves as people and it is always possible that they will be rejected. They are not able to fall back on control and power.

Authority by influence works at building a relationship with a child based on trust. The adult trusts the child to behave in acceptable ways, and the adult works to earn the trust of the child. At times the adult will be undeserving of the child's trust, and vice versa, but authority by influence assumes that the relationship will be preserved because of the genuine care and concern the adult and child have for each other. Because both the adult and child are vulnerable to one another, one's behavior can cause the other not only joy but pain.

Authority by influence is so relationship-oriented that it does not strive for justification or confirmation in the eyes of observers. Maintaining this kind of relationship requires a tremendous commitment of time and energy; it is very gradual in development. However, it is longlasting and the adult involved in such a relationship need not worry about ever being fired. An authority by influence has a permanent position. Many an adult is already an authority by influence; many others are striving towards that goal.

3

"I wish you'd stop hitting me! I hate you!"

"It hurts me more than it hurts you to have to spank you."

"Then don't do it!"

"Yeah but, children need

Discipline

THE CONCEPT OF discipline is best understood when viewed as an extension of the types of authority already discussed. What can authority figures do when the recipient of their authority rejects either control efforts or influence?

For people who use authority to control, "discipline" is a verb meaning something done *to* the child when authority is rejected; for people who use authority to influence, "discipline" is a noun meaning the repertoire of behaviors a child is helped to develop *within* himself/herself.

Control authority figures assume that after enough discipline has been *imposed* on the child, inner-directed self-discipline will emerge. In other words, control authority figures emphasize and rely upon the verb aspect of discipline; they assume that the noun aspect either develops concomitantly or in the child's later years. The underlying assumptions and implications for both kinds of discipline need to be scrutinized.

DISCIPLINE AND AUTHORITY BY CONTROL

Meeting Adults' Needs. Adults who exert their authority by control or power are fulfilling some individual and personal need. As suggested in the preceeding chapter, such adults are usually concerned with the observable effects of their interactions with children; generally they are not particularly interested in what these children are feeling.

Many times this need for immediate results forces adults to be less than honest about why they seek certain behavior from children. Many adults make flat statements such as "No, you cannot do that because you might get hurt," which at first glance seems to reflect concern for the child's well-being. However, many times the adult is using this concern to avoid another potentially annoying situation.

Consider the example of an adult telling a child that he/she may not go over to the neighborhood playground because he/she might get hurt. Perhaps what the adult really means is "I don't feel like going over there now and playing with you." Afraid to work these feelings through with the child, the adult disguises his/her true feelings under the guise of concern. Meanwhile the child, sitting out front watching the other kids playing at the playground, has yet to see anyone get hurt, and is old enough to know that one can get injured just as easily walking down a flight of stairs in the house as whizzing down the slide. The child feels deceived and resentful when he/she gets the "I did it for your own good" routine.

In such situations the adult usually feels satisfied, at least initially, because he/she has been obeyed. Of course, the child's pent up rage can surface in other ways and create future problems. Furthermore, continual circumventing of the real issues by certain adults causes children to become distrustful of adults' warnings. A child does not have to be very mature to see through such attempts at manipulation. I have heard children as young as three or four respond to such a situation with, "Oh, sure. You just want me to stay home."

Another example of discipline being used to meet an adult's needs involves the forcing of activities on kids. "You *will* practice the piano, it is good discipline and you'll thank me when you get older" may in reality be a cover-up for "I wish I knew how to play the piano because then I would have something to offer at the Friday night parties." In short, the relationship between discipline and authority by control must be considered in terms of adult needs being met in the name of children's welfare.

It has been suggested that adults who assert their authority via control and power often have a need to gain peer approval; they behave in ways that they hope will result in their looking good or at least effective in the eyes of other adults. Sometimes they come on tough in the presence of children, to make a "See what lies in store for you if you act up" point. They are always very aware of those around them. This probably helps explain why many adults will absolutely devastate a child for misbehaving in a roomful of people rather than extending the courtesy of dealing with the child privately. Many times the rationale offered is, "I just couldn't let this go until later. It was so serious that it required my immediate attention. Ah, things would be so much easier if I didn't care about that child so much...."

I have witnessed this scene too many times. (I might agree that the child has misbehaved, but I feel resentment towards adults who draw me into these situations.) I sit dumbly, staring at my lap, nervously gnawing at my lower lip while waiting for this totally embarrassing and unpleasant scene to be over. Occasionally my eyes meet those of the child being ranted and raved at, and I inevitably look back to my lap. The terror and pleading in his/her eyes make me feel so helpless!

This is not to suggest that the child in this hypothetical but familiar situation is being unjustly accused of unacceptable behavior. This is not at issue here. It can be assumed that the child has behaved in a way distressing and upsetting to the adult and that the behavior must be dealt with. What is at issue is how many adults have a need to perform in front of other people as they discipline a child. It is troublesome to know what to do when we end up in the audience during such scenes.

I know what I will do in the future. Rather than pretending that nothing is going on or making my usual attempts at joviality after the scene has ended, I will leave the room. I will hope that my presence is missed enough that the adult interacting with the child will question me about my departure. In the future I will want him/ her to know what I was feeling and why I did not want to be a part of the conflict. When friends tell me during such scenes, "Oh stay. You're like one of the family," I will make it very clear that at the moment I do not feel like being a member of that family and why.

Mind Your Own Business! The preceding situation raises the question of why observing adults feel reluctant to intercede when another adult is interacting with a child in such a destructive way. There is apparently an unwritten and rarely discussed assumption that parents *own* their children; children are possessions. Few of us react if an adult gets upset with a car and starts abusing it. "That's his car. If he wants to bang it up, that's *his* business." Many of us extend this kind of reasoning to children. "That's his kid. If he wants to abuse him that's none of my business." Why else would we observe rough treatment of a child and pretend that it isn't happening? We do not like to interfere, and those who do interfere are looked at askance, to say the least.

A few years ago I was supervising a group of student teachers. One day we were all in one of the large exhibit halls of a museum trying to talk and be heard over the yelling of a child of about three. The mother was obviously upset with this child; her own yelling was promptly matched by the little boy. All of a sudden one of my student teachers, without a word to anyone, strode across the room, scooped the child up in her arms, said some comforting words to him and carried him over to a display a few feet away. While they were chatting the mother gaped at them with her mouth ajar. I was across the room saying to myself, "Gwen, we'll all end up in jail." A few minutes later Gwen deposited a very calm child back with his mother and returned to us.

I was too dumbfounded to respond to what had just happened and I let pass a beautiful opportunity for discussion. Gwen didn't say a word about it and we all pretended the whole thing hadn't happened. But it had happened. Gwen had behaved as many of us fantasize about behaving. The mother and little boy went happily from display to display. Their crisis had passed because a young woman had recognized a situation where she could pitch in and help both an adult and a child. May the rest of us learn from the Gwens of the world.

There is a risk involved in trying to help out in a situation between an adult and a child, especially if one is a stranger. Once I was standing in line to be checked out in a busy drugstore. I had an armful of stuff and the line was moving slowly. Behind me were a mother and little boy. The waiting was obviously a chore for him. He was whining and squirming all over the place while his mother was telling him to shape up and stand still. When it was my turn at the register I told the mother to go ahead of me.

She thanked me but said no, he would have to learn to be patient. I insisted she go next and she reiterated the little boy's need to learn patience. There I was feeling rejected on a Saturday morning in a busy drugstore. I wanted to scream, "But he isn't learning patience. He is learning to resent you because you aren't doing everything possible to help him out. He heard me offer to let you go first. I would like you to go first. It would make me feel good to do that." Instead I smiled demurely. By the time I finally got through the line and out, that little boy was all but thrashing on the floor with exhaustion. Patience, indeed!

Another reason why adults hesitate to intercede in a harsh situation between an adult and a child is simple unadulterated fear. The reasoning goes something like this: "If that adult would talk to a child that way, who know what he/she would say to me!" It is reassuring to know that as adults we have this option to protect our psyches from possible attack, but it is important to acknowledge how this element of fear operates. Its potential effects make us ignore certain situations which aren't "any of our business anyway." If we see someone about to step in front of an oncoming car we are more apt to intercede because we can visualize the result if we ignore the situation. Psychological damage is less objective and involves individual values about how we like to see children treated.

The best an interceding adult can hope to do is help relieve the tension of a given situation; it is unlikely that this will serve as a springboard for genuine attempts at change. The feelings of helplessness that both children and adults experience during such exchanges are neither unrealistic nor exaggerated, but they seem basic to authority by control and power. Feelings of helplessness, dependency, and fear on the part of the recipient are prerequisites for the success of discipline by control.

Learning Appropriate Behavior. Obviously, all infants are initially helpless and dependent upon adults for the fulfillment of their most basic needs. As they get older some children exhibit independent behavior earlier than other children; some children remain helpless and dependent long after they have acquired the maturational tools to behave in more independent ways; some adults depend on others to meed their needs. How do we account for such variations in personality?

In *Childhood and Society,* psycho-historian Erik Erikson describes eight stages we move through in personality formation. The first of these is Basic Trust vs. Basic Mistrust, and like other writers, e.g., William Homan (1969) and Lee Salk (1973), Erikson stresses the importance of trust being established for the infant.

> The infant's first social achievement is his willingness to let the mother out of sight without undue anxiety or rage, because she has become an inner certainty as well as an outer predictability (Erikson, p. 247).

This stage is followed by Autonomy vs. Shame and Doubt. Erikson suggests that

> Too much shaming does not lead to genuine propriety but to a secret determination to try to get away with things, unseen—if, indeed, it does not result in defiant shamelessness. (p. 253).

The third stage is described as Initiative vs. Guilt. Erkison feels that it is during this time, usually around ages three to five, that the child is at a peak for quick and avid learning.

> He is eager and able to make things cooperatively, to combine with other children for the purpose of constructing and planning, and he is willing to profit from teachers and to emulate ideal prototypes (p. 258).

It is probably during this stage of development that the child is first susceptible to the effects of guilt. The child becomes aware of new locomotor and mental powers while at the same time being aware of the expectations of people in the environment who are important. Parents cannot help but be cognizant of their child's exuberance, endless activity, and efforts at establishing self-will. It is at this time that adults who use authority to control often instill in the child a sense of guilt in order to try to channel the child's limitless energy. The child seeks acceptance but is pulled in a myriad of directions as he/she interacts with the environment. The child's efforts to move from one activity to the next, to manipulate objects in the environment, and to grow mentally and emotionally are often thwarted with such statements as "You are naughty," or "A good girl or boy wouldn't do that."

The child wants and needs acceptance from adults and after hearing such admonishments for a period of time, he/she begins to feel remorseful, culpable, and unself-confident. The child's innate sense of initiative is affected by guilt feelings—sometimes to the point of incapacitation. The child is compelled to move from activity to activity and is also compelled to seek acceptance. The two are not always compatible in terms of acceptable behavior. During these early years the guilt feelings a child may be experiencing are an inevitable outgrowth of a natural development.

However, deliberately instilling feelings of guilt in children is sometimes used to manipulate behavior. The child misbehaves and the adult needs and wants to deal with this misbehavior. Older children's increased ability to comprehend language and its nuances is recognized; some adults make a conscious effort to implant guilt feelings; "You ought to be ashamed of yourself." "How could you do that after all we have done for you?" Comments such as these are deliberate attempts to demean the child, to specifically arouse guilt about behaving in a certain way. They work.

The child does not feel good about himself/herself, fears rejection, and often resorts to manipulative behavior to dissipate these feelings. If guilt is cultivated over a long enough period of time the child learns not only that he/she is an unworthy and insignificant person, but also how to avoid having to interact with the people who generate these feelings in him/her. Hence, a ceasing of sharing with those adults—a communication breakdown.

The issue is further complicated by many children's constant striving to be individuals while receiving concentrated doses of guilt. Hence, defiance and rebellion. The child's internal forces compel survival in an atmosphere which is trying to beat him/her down. Trying to make another person feel guilty is a nasty business indeed. We all do it at one time or another, and we all somehow pay a price. If we persist in using guilt as a tool to control another person, it is only logical that we understand the implications of our actions.

Dealing With Unacceptable Behavior: Punishment. Doling out punishment is a way of instilling feelings of guilt. A punishment is a way of telling someone that he/she is a failure and must pay a price. If the child genuinely cares about the adult giving out the punishment, feelings of guilt are inevitable. The child wants to be accepted by this person, cares about the adult, and in turn cares what the adult thinks of him/her. If a child is a failure in the eyes of a meaningful adult, guilt and feelings of "I am not a worthwhile person" result. If the child does not care about the adult administering the punishment, the whole thing becomes a ritual to be endured, a game that must be played. Feigned remorse and profuse apologies become standard props.

Many times punishment is used as a disciplinary method simply because the adult doesn't know what else to do. It is the result of frustration. The adult really cares about the child, and, feeling a sense of responsibility, is compelled to do something. More often than not this something is punishment. Something is done to the child in hopes that the child will see the "error" and mend his/her ways.

Punishment is just another attempt at controlling someone else's behavior; unfortunately, the punishment is often decided in the heat of anger. "Open your mouth once more and you'll stay in an extra week." The child is angry too, and sometimes fights to get the last word in. In this climate the punishment keeps getting harsher and harsher and it is questionable whether a child can move from his/her resentment of the whole process into an evaluation of the offensive behavior.

It is more expedient for many children to just say what the adult in control wants to hear: "Oh yes. I can see that what I did was wrong. I am so sorry". True thoughts such as "OH, FLAKE OFF! I am so sick and tired of you" never get aired. The price to be paid is a phony and insincere relationship with the child's primary concern being not to get caught. The obedience is a facade masking an internal concern with conniving and outsmarting the controlling authority.

Spanking is probably the most destructive punishment in terms of what a child really learns from it. Many children will opt for a spanking simply because it is quick and parents seem to feel so much better after it is over. An article in a popular women's magazine entitled "What Parents Should Know About Punishing Their Children," (Norman Lobsenz, 1972), concluded that punishment simply doesn't work. Parents punish for themselves, as a kind of catharsis, even though they suspect it doesn't work. The article never questions the effects of punishment on the parent-child relationship, nor does it offer alternatives to punishment. The author merely wants readers to be aware that it ultimately doesn't work.

I would like to suggest that it *does* work, but in negative and unanticipated ways. A child can learn all kinds of things from a spanking. He/she can learn that hitting is a right sanctioned for adults, inflicting pain on others is permissible as long as you are bigger than the person you are hitting, and force must be the only way to settle disagreements between adults and children. (An adult hitting a child is administering a spanking—acceptable. A child doing the same thing to another child is hitting—unacceptable.) It is particularly distressing and ironic to watch a kid being told, while getting a whaling for hitting a younger sibling, "I don't even want to catch you hitting your younger brother/sister again or I will give you a spanking you'll never forget!" This is utterly confusing for a child. When children model the hitting they see their parents do, and try too to use it as a method of resolution, they get hit.

I remember spanking our daughter when she was about 18 months old. I was trying to change her diaper and she was squirming like an eel. I lost my patience and walloped her on her fanny. She bolted upright, looked me square in the eye, and whacked me back on the arm. My instant thinking "How dare you strike me, your mother?" fortunately changed quickly to "Whoa. What is really going on here?" I apologized to her, put her down on the floor and told her I was so enraged with her squirming that I needed to be away from her. She stayed in her room while I fumed around the living room. A few minutes later I went in, picked her up and changed her.

I am glad Heather took that swipe at me. I was able to get by the whole issue of how she lacked respect for me and how I shouldn't let her get away with that kind of behavior. Of course she didn't respect me. How can anyone respect someone who treats him/her in such a demeaning way? I could demand and get fear out of her, but certainly not respect. She helped me realize the futility of using spanking to work through a disagreeable situation.

Many parents have made the comment that there are times when spanking is justified, for example, when teaching a child not to step off a curb into the street unattended. I used to believe this but I have seen too many children who have been spanked back to the curb dart out into the street in the absence of the spanker. It seems apparent that the spankee has learned to expect a spanking but has not gained an appreciation of the real consequences of crossing the street unattended. It appears to be more effective to spend great amounts of time at the curb with the child repeating over and over again why the adult worries about the child crossing the street alone. This is incredibly time-consuming but it works. Children can learn the difference between darting away from a spanking and darting into the path of cars that can hurt them.

Oftentimes the phenomenon of punishment becomes an end in itself. Somewhere along the line adults lose sight of what the punishment is supposed to be accomplishing. They get bogged down in deciding the punishment, executing it, and making sure it is carried out. If, say, a child has been sent to his/her room as a punishment and the parent has to go out, often a sibling is asked to report back to the parent whether or not the culprit actually fulfilled the punishment. (The coded message is, "If you couldn't be trusted to behave correctly in the first place, you certainly cannot be trusted to carry out your punishment." This type of an assignment puts the reporting sibling in an awkward position.)

Many times kids will weasle or finagle their way out of the punishment. The punisher forgets that the child was to be grounded at a given time and the child gets called on the carpet for not taking the punishment even though the punisher forgot about it. The adult is right in feeling that the punishment was not being taken seriously, but the point is that often we get so mired down in the punishment game that we forget what it was originally designed to do. At some point many adults realize this but they do not know any alternative forms of discipline.

To complicate matters, many adults are so into the punishment method that they are unable to reverse or re-evaluate a punishment once it has been decreed. The adult is probably striving for consistency and respect which makes it impossible for him/her to say to the child, "Hey look. I was really upset when I said you had to do such and such for a punishment. I've had a chance to cool off and simmer down and I can see that I was being unfair." Many adults view such a position as a sign of weakness and indecisiveness rather than as an opportunity to accept humanness and to work on building a relationship with a child. The punishment becomes the issue and often loses its supposed role as a vehicle to change and growth.

Then there are those adults who are admittedly uncomfortable with the method of punishment. They feel intuitively that it is ineffective and ultimately destructive, but again, they have not been given any relationship-building skills that make it possible to abandon punishment as a disciplinary method. Many such adults attempt to be democratic in doling out punishments and some writers even encourage this approach.

> What the child wants is to feel not only that you are an authority and strong and in a position to mandate punishments, but also that you are warm and protective at the same time and loving enough to negotiate the degree of punishment (Salk, p. 40).

I question that children are really looking for authority figures to mandate punishments. Parents and child alike suggest that this is not so.* It seems contradictory to talk about a person being in the powerful position of mandating punishments while at the same time being warm and protective. I suggest, in a sense facetiously and yet seriously, that what children need protection

*A neighbor once told me of receiving an anniversary card from her 11-year-old daughter in which she thanked her parents for spanking her. She knew it was only because they loved her that they spanked her. Her mother was "thrilled and delighted" because her own daughter reinforced that they were doing the right thing. It is safe to assume that this thrill and delight was relayed to the child.

from is the type of adults who mandate punishments. "Would you rather be flogged or stoned, my child?" This is supposed to help children learn decision-making processes, but it is absurd. It puts the child in a very unrealistic and awkward position. Here is a child who is seeking acceptance from an adult while being asked to decide on his/her own punishment. The child wants to come up with something that is harsh enough to suggest to the adult that the opportunity is appreciated and that he/she recognizes the seriousness of misbehaving while at the same time, trying to think of something that is not going to be too painful.

If the emphasis is supposed to be on decision-making skills, it would seem more reasonable to have the adult and child make some decisions about, the whole realm of punishment. Salk (1973) writes, "I think it is better to get the child to enter into the decision first, then let the parents enforce it (p. 40)." The title of the article is "What Decisions Parents Should Allow Children To Make." The answer seems to be, Any They Can Enforce.

Discipline Without Tyranny, a book by Loren Grey (1972), caught my eye a few years ago. The author describes a method of discipline called "logical consequences." "A child who refuses to eat isn't scolded. After a reasonable period of time, his food is removed and he goes unfed until the next mealtime." Another example: a child wants to stay up later than his/her usual bedtime. No scene ensues. The child is allowed to stay up and then gotten up the next morning at the regular rising time. The idea is that a child must see the relationship between what he/she does and the consequence of doing it. The child is always given a choice between what he/she wants to do and what he/she should do.

I see this as sophisticated manipulation without any concern for the needs motivating the child's closen behavior. This approach deals with observable behavior, but not with the cause of it. Again, children are being asked to make responses from a predetermined list of choices, and this is supposed to be constructive because the child knows beforehand the logical consequences of personal behavior.

The use of punishment does more to destroy an adult-child relationship than any other factor. Allowing children the "privilege" to participate in the punishment game is demeaning to all involved. If it is used consistently during a child's formative years, communication between adult and child is often of a cold war nature by the time the teen years roll around. Both parties are totally frustrated and life becomes just a series of hassles which promote neither learning nor growing.

Many children start living for the day when they can get away and be on their own, and the pity of it is that they have received very little guidance and support for this independence. Many times a relationship has deteriorated to such an extent that even the involved adults are secretly fantasizing about the day when the child will actually pack up and leave. The children feel guilty about harboring such negative feelings towards these adults, usually their parents, and the adults in turn are left with guilty feelings about their failures in interacting with the children. These kinds of experiences can ultimately affect each party's abilities to function in day-to-day living. Many people who have experienced such a disintegrating relationship feel unfulfilled, bitter, depressed, and guilty.

A fundamental question is: Can children behave responsibly and cooperatively in the absence of punishment? After all, we all like to interact with responsible children and we want to raise responsible children. Children's misbehavior and the problems that arise when they are assigned household chores suggest that many of us are not succeeding in raising what we consider responsible children. Barbara Park points out how many children who are considered irresponsible in their own homes behave in miraculously responsible ways in other people's homes. Parents enjoy hearing from friends and neighbors that their child "is such a joy to have around. He/she is always so willing to help out," but it is often a source of concern and puzzlement that they don't behave this way at home.

However, is getting a job done what is important to the child? It is very possible that in the absence of nagging, prodding, and threats in someone else's home, children easily achieve unconditional acceptance from the adults present. There is no threat of punishment hanging over their heads, so they are able to pitch in merely to reap the rewards of good feelings, to get the strokes.

Parents sometimes have to fight a lonely battle in helping children become responsible. One author gives an example citing his son. The son says: "Why can't I go to the drugstore by myself after school? Everybody goes there." The father responds: "Everybody may, but the drugstore is across heavily-travelled Connecticut Avenue and school lets out shortly before the evening rush hour begins." This makes sense and would probably seem very reasonable to a youngster, but the author adds, "Moreover, there is nothing at a large busy drugstore that a healthy ten-year-old boy really needs (Shannon, p. 38)."

The first point about the traffic is valid, but it is questionable how accepting this young boy will remain about having his needs defined for him by his father. Further on the author says, "It takes courage and determination to administer a spanking, to say 'no,' to set rules and stick by them (p. 38)." If we are going to talk about responsibility being developed in children, I would rather see the quotation read, "It takes short-sightedness and insensitivity to administer a spanking; it takes courage and determination to say 'let's talk about it,' to set rules together, and be willing to re-evaluate and discuss them."

DISCIPLINE AND AUTHORITY BY INFLUENCE

Rita Kramer (1969a) reviewed numerous articles in women's magazines written in the 1940s and 1950s and concluded that

The emphasis in these articles always seems to be on not breaking a child's will—assumed to be a very fragile thing—rather than on teaching him to control it (p. 93).

Kramer speculates that this shift in child-rearing practices was related to a post-World War II atmosphere in which freedom was very important to people. A parent who had unquestioned obedience from a child was thought to have raised a Nazi. Over and over again the articles seemed to emphasize a child's need for love, but this was never differentiated from indulgence.

Adults interacting with children today face the same dilemma: should they use authority by control or permissiveness? This doesn't have to be an either/or situation—authority-by-influence is another option. Authority by influence does not call for kids being "Spocked when they should have been spanked (Kramer, p. 93)," nor is it a compromise between the two. What is being suggested is an approach to authority and discipline which is effective and yet strengthens relationships instead of chipping away at them.

People practicing authority by influence do not ask for immediate observable changes in children's behavior. They are willing to invest a great deal of time and patience in their interactions, knowing that permanent and meaningful change is gradual and oftentimes eludes observation. They deal with feelings and emotions— their own and those of the involved children. They would tell the youngster who wanted to go over to the playground, for example, that they really couldn't gather up the energy or enthusiasm for going over to the playground right then. Hopefully, an adult would have the skills both to say this in an unthreatening way and to work through the conflict until there was satisfaction on both sides. These exchanges require time and patience. The investment is well worth it as it keeps the relationship intact. Openness and honesty are fundamental concepts, but for many they remain just terms. Applying these concepts in their daily lives is difficult for people who have never really tried to before.

An adult attempting to really interact with a child's feelings is not concerned with peer approval. He/she simply doesn't need it. To this type of adult, it is the message relayed to the child that counts first and foremost in their relationship. This is not always so easy to put into practice.

We go back again to Ben. Ben is the seven-year old son of a good friend who, with him, has recently learned the kinds of skills under discussion here. I also have been attempting to interact with Ben using these skills and he knows it! He is skeptical of our attempts because all of a sudden he is being asked to trust us and to give us his trust. He is not really sure at this point that he *can* trust us. Ben is periodically trying to trip us up as we interact with him so that he can say, "See. What you're trying to do just doesn't work."

One day I was over at the local pool with Ben when he apparently decided it was time to test me. He started ranting and raving at me that I hadn't paid him back the nickel I had borrowed from him a few days before. I told him that he was absolutely right, that I had been forgetful and I would pay him back as soon as I got home. Ben kept up a running tirade about how he had to have that nickel right then and there and how I was taking advantage of him just because he was a kid.

It was at this point I became very aware of the audience staring at the two of us. We had become the center of the entire poolside scene. I had such thoughts as, "You obnoxious kid, putting me in this ridiculous position. Everyone is looking at me." I knew that what was expected of me. I was supposed to put this kid in his place and terminate the nickel business, and I knew I had the power to do so. Fortunately, something kept rumbling around inside of me; I had an inkling he wanted me to use my big guns just to prove a point to himself. I finally yelled at him that I was too upset to discuss it right then and I wandered over to the other side of the pool and sat down.

Lo and behold! Who should come wandering over right behind me? Ben sat beside me as I told him that I didn't appreciate being treated that way; I just didn't consider that any way to treat a friend. He smiled, somewhat devilishly I think, and said that he was wondering what I would do. We talked some more and he ended by telling me to forget about the nickel. My reward, I suppose, for my not pulling a power play on him. Remind me never to borrow money from Ben again. I have to work too hard for the loan!

The point is that I was very aware of the surrounding people watching us and I was aware of the temptation to put Ben down. I could have disguised it by saying he was being disrespectful of an adult, or I could have said something subtle like, "Your parents wouldn't appreciate knowing how rude you have been." I do consider Ben a friend and I know he likes me. We have a good relationship, and we both have to work at it. Sometimes one of us might tend to be a bit nasty or inconsiderate, but we can talk about that, too. Come to think of it, I haven't felt that Ben has been testing me for months now!

It was suggested in an earlier example that because adults do not always understand a child's needs or know how to interact in such a way as to learn about these needs, the "You may not do such and such" approach creates all kinds of additional problems for both the child and the adult. The example of the child who wanted to go down to the drugstore is relevant. The father, an advocate of spanking, told his son that there was no good reason to want to go to the drugstore after school. The father's response was a flat NO. I suggest that this kind of interaction often results in the child's sneaking around and lying about his/her actual whereabouts. It can be assumed that the adult in the example had some very valid apprehensions about the child going to that particular place and it can also be assumed that the child had some equally valid reasons for wanting to go there.

Both parties in a relationship have some very real needs. With appropriate communication skills these needs can be aired and dealt with. Again it is emphasized that this process often requires time and patience. If the child knows that his/her needs are being genuinely considered, there is no need for sneaking or lying to get around punishments. Each party accepts the other's needs even if he/she doesn't agree with them. For example, the child may consider it foolish of the adult to worry about the posibility of getting hurt, but he/she can accept that the adult is truly concerned. If the initial resolution of the conflict does not satisfy both parties' needs, they know they will have to sit down and go over the process again, step by step, and arrive at another resolution. This may require several repetitions over a period of time. Rather than sneaking behind the adult's back, all the child has to do is say, "Hey, this just isn't working. What are we going to do about it?" The adult has the same option.

Meanwhile the child is learning inner discipline. He/she is learning how to uphold one end of a bargain and to follow through on an agreement; how to enter into a decision-making process; how to take into account another person's needs; how to deal with the give and take of a relationship; and how to accept the responsibility of working at a relationship to make it grow. A party might feel guilty about not upholding the proper share of the relationship, but no one would have to worry about the other trying to make him/her feel guilty. A person might say, "I am really disappointed that you didn't do such and such," but not with the intent of dumping a wagon-load of guilt on the other person.

Sharing such feelings merely lets the other person know that "I care about what we are trying to do and when you behave in such and such a way, it makes me feel that you don't care." This puts the responsibility of modifying behavior on the other person. Because both parties care about each other and their relationship, each is intrinsically motivated to re-evaluate all behaviors involved.

Authority-by-control and its related discipline tend to work with isolated bits of behavior so it is hard to generalize their application to other situations. Authory-by-influence and *its* related discipline do lend themselves to generalization. Picking things up around the house or classroom after they have been used is a common problem. Our Heather uses crayons quite frequently. It is not uncommon for them to be all over the living room floor when she is through playing with them. When she was younger I would pick them up and ask her if she would please help me. Sometimes she would and other times she wouldn't. When she would not help me I would pick them up, but I would tell her that I needed to have them off the carpet because they could get ground in and ruin it and that I didn't appreciate having to clean up her mess. When she *would* help me I would tell her that I appreciated her cooperation and it made me feel really good inside that she could be so responsible.

This is a process that went on for months and there were times I wanted to shake her and scream, "Pick up your damn crayons!" Instead I would pick them up while explaining how I felt she was really taking advantage of me and that I didn't feel she was doing her share of the household work. She'd follow me around hanging on my every word. Now she not only picks up her crayons when she is done using them, but she puts other toys away and hangs her sweaters and jackets on her hooks without my having to ask her. There are still times when she won't, but they are infrequent. When I do pick up after her I tell her something like, "I can see that you are not in the mood to pick up your things. Well, I want you to know that I don't feel like it either, but I can't have this stuff hanging around getting ruined and having to be replaced. That would waste time and money."

I do not feel that I am letting her get away with anything because I do see growth in terms of responsibility and I see her generalize this growth to other areas—there is no question about it. I could, at any given time, after much unpleasantness, make her pick up her stuff, but I know that I will pay for her resentment. She could become completely uncooperative all the time and I just do not want to face a battle each and every time things have to be straightened up. I also feel that by handling the situation this way I am telling her, "Hey, you can have your lazy mood or whatever it is that prevents you from helping out. I accept that, but I sure don't like it." It is more important to me to have Heather as a friend and to be a friend to Heather than it is to have her pick up her crayons.

To be friends with a daughter? This is our goal. However, it is only recently that we considered this a desirable goal. Somewhere along the way I picked up the idea that one could never be both a parent and a friend to one's own child. One could never be both a teacher and a friend to one's students. I held to this idea tenaciously for years and years, though I cannot pinpoint its origin. Now I am convinced that an adult can be nothing positive to a child unless he/she is *first* accepted as a friend.

It becomes apparent that the inner, self-directed kind of discipline described here would be stifled by punishment. In a relationship-oriented approach to developing discipline, punishment would hamper the relationship and if used enough could even terminate it. Parties involved in this type of relationship certainly share feelings of disappointment and rejection, but they are shared in an atmosphere of "This is what *I* am feeling as a result of interacting with you. Do you care enough to want to help me deal with them?" The other party does not have to grapple with feeling unworthwhile and insignificant as a person. He/she is merely made aware of the fact that his/her behavior has made some kind of an impact on the other person.

Both are influenced by what the other has done, but neither's self-esteem is under attack. The relationship is founded on trust and both parties are motivated by this trust to get on with the business of preserving and enhancing the relationship. There is no place for control, power, or punishment in this kind of an interaction.

Self-Esteem and Discipline. There is a lack of hard data on the correlation between children's feelings of self-worth or self-esteem and parental attitudes towards authority and discipline. One researcher has focused on self-esteem and some of his findings are of interest here. Psychologist Stanley Coopersmith (1968) conducted an eight-year longitudinal study in self-esteem. He followed a representative sample of normal boys from pre-adolescence through early adulthood. The boys were urban, middle-class, and showed no pathological personality disturbances. They were first asked to give personal estimations of their self-esteem. Additional indices used were the Rorschach Test and the TAT (Thematic Apperception Test) which indicated a person's unconscious self-evaluation. Also, teachers who had worked with the boys rated them. More than 80 percent of the ratings by these indices were substantially in accord with each boy's individual estimate of his self-esteem. The boys were then grouped as either high, medium, or low in self-esteem.

> We found, not very surprisingly, that youngsters with a high degree of self-esteem were active, expressive individuals who tend to be successful both academically and socially...They approach other people with the expectation that they will be well received (Coopersmith, p.98)

It was found that the boys in the middle level of self-esteem

> showed the strongest tendency to support the middle-class value system and compliance with its norms and demands. They were also the most uncertain in their self-ratings of their personal worth and tended to be particularly dependent on social acceptance (Coopersmith, p. 98).

Coopersmith notes that many interesting findings resulted from looking into the backgrounds of the boys possessing high self-esteem. It was found that these boys had close relationships with their parents and that their parents' love was reflected in an interest in their sons' welfare, concern about their sons' friends, and "availability for discussion of the boys' problems and participation in congenial joint activities (p. 99)."

Another finding was more surprising. The inquiry into the boys' backgrounds suggested that the parents of the high self-esteem boys tended to be less permissive than those of children with low self-esteem. The parents of the high self-esteem boys

> demanded high standards of behavior and were strict and consistent in enforcement of the rules. Yet their discipline was by no means harsh; indeed, these parents were less punitive than the parents of the boys whom we found to be lacking in self-esteem. They used rewards rather than corporal punishment or withdrawal of love as disciplinary techniques, and their sons praised their fairness (Coopersmith, p. 99).

Coopersmith describes these parents as presiding as "benevolent despots"; they accepted dissent, were open to persuasion by their children, and were willing to allow the children the right to participate in family decisions. In short,

> It seems safe to conclude that all these factors—deep interest in the children, the guidance provided by well-defined rules of expected behavior, non-punitive treatment and respect for the children's views—contributed greatly to the development of the boys' high self-esteem (Coopersmith p. 100).

It is imperative that such research be continued and expanded. It is of the utmost importance for adults who interact with children to know in other than intuitive ways what effects they are having or might be having.

An adult practicing authority-by-influence acts as a source of support and guidance. This role often requires the adult to hold back, that is, not to intercede in the activities of a child, even when the adult feels that he/she has *the* answer to a situation. Educator Carl Bereiter (1973) makes the point that it seems that almost all people in the helping professions—educators, social workers, psychologists, psychiatrists, and I add parents to the list—operate on "a deeply-rooted conviction that people should not be allowed to make mistakes (p. 190)." Further, Bereiter stresses that all people, including children, have the right to make mistakes, and that "A right is something a person is entitled to whether he uses it wisely or not (p. 190)."

It was adhering to this belief which made it possible for me to watch Heather taste her feces while toilet-training. I saw her scoop some out of her potty-seat and I even anticipated what was coming next. I could have prevented her from putting it in her mouth *that* time, but as I suspected that she would only try to do it another time I accepted her need to taste it. As her feces-laden finger was making its way up to her mouth I said, "I know you probably will not want to take my word for it, but 'poop' doesn't taste good. " In it went and just as quickly out it come.

When I told a friend about it he was absolutely repulsed and wanted to know how I could possibly let her do that. We talked about it until we were both satisfied that Heather was just executing her right to make mistakes. My telling her that something was a mistake could never be as meaningful as her finding out firsthand. These kinds of experiences also make her more susceptible to my judgmental influences and help her to learn at which points in her decision-making she might want to seek some advice. I feel confident that tasting poop today means inner, self-directed discipline tomorrow. And NO, I would not let Heather step in front of an oncoming car in the name of letting her make her own mistakes.

The discipline which people using authority-by-influence try to foster in children is a set of behaviors which are utilized even in the absence of adult company. The child learns acceptable and encouraged behavior in one situation, and in the absence of threats and punishments experiments with applying this behavior in other situations. This kind of approach to discipline is time consuming and immediate effects are usually minimal. It is a gradual process of growth and change. The most important goal of the parties involved is the preservation of their relationship. The authority figure neither seeks nor needs peer approval because the only concern is with what is happening between the two people in the relationship. This approach to discipline deals with feelings and emotions. The underlying message is, "I need to know how my interacting with you is affecting you, and I want you to know how your interacting with me is affecting me."

Both the child and the adult possess the potential to influence the other's feelings and ultimately behavior, because they genuinely care about each other. It is this caring in an open, honest, and accepting climate which allows for inner, self-initiated discipline. There are peaks and valleys in communications, and emotions will run the gamut, but the relationship will be preserved.

4

"I'm sorry, but you will go."
"Sunday school is so boring. I hate it!"
"Yeah but, children need

Morals And Values

WHAT IS GOODNESS? What is the right thing to do? What is justice? Questions such as these have been the source of thought, debate, and controversy since the emergence of language. Today the topics can take such forms as Watergate, violence in society, or a seven-year-old child stealing a candy bar from the local drugstore. I certainly have no intentions or hopes of answering questions such as these. Instead, the emphasis here is on some of the roles morals and values play in interactions with children.

Why do so many children resist adult codes of moral behavior? Why, when they become young adults, do so many adopt and live by ethical codes which seem alien to all we have tried to teach them as children? Questions such as these cause much pain and anxiety for adults, especially parents.

Moral behavior is concerned with the distinction between right and wrong. Adjectives describing moral behavior include righteous, just, upright, straightforward, open, and honest. *Morals as a code of behavior* refers to generally accepted customs of conduct in society, and to the individual's behavior in relation to them.

Values refer to the ideals, customs, and institutions which the people of a society hold desirable as means or as ends in themselves. A value has worth which implies intrinsic excellence or desirability. So states the dictionary.

We can easily say that honesty is a value in our society, but then how do we explain so much of the dishonest behavior we observe when this value is translated into actual practice? We can define the values or attributes that we like to see in people, but something seems to happen when individuals develop their own moral codes of behavior. Even though there seems to be agreement as to what some of our social values might be, we observe much divergent and diverse behavior as people strive to incorporate these values into their own lives. For purposes of this discussion it is perhaps helpful to think of *values* as a noun referring to qualities and attributes, and *moral behavior* as a verb describing the action taken in an attempt to implement values.

It is tempting to conclude that people who behave in ways which are contrary to our own moral behavior are immoral, suggesting that they are wicked, depraved, and licentious. With behaviors such as murder we can be very comfortable with this conclusion. However, we usually resist the temptation to conclude that people engaged in less heinous behaviors are immoral, especially if they are people we know and love. It is common to throw our hands up in the air, and conclude that we just don't understand them.

This is especially common in relationships between parents and children. "How can you possibly go on a weekend camping trip where there will be both girls and boys together and no adult supervision?" Both the adult and the young adult value decency, but living up to this value can take different paths. Some parents would conclude that their teenager is immoral to go off on this unsupervised weekend, but most parents would react with such thoughts as, "I know my son/daughter is not immoral, but how do I explain such behavior? I just don't understand it." The adult is perplexed.

THE NATURE OF MAN*

Psychologist C. W. Graves (1966) feels that many view the nature of man based on a premise consisting of three parts:

1. That beneath it all man is a beast driven by original sin, aggressiveness, and a death instinct.
2. That civilized human behavior, good values, can only be superimposed on man and therefore must be constantly imposed upon him lest his animalism override his humanism.
3. That these good values, Judeo-Christian ethics, Buddhist principles or the like, have been revealed to man and are the prime tenets by which he should live.

This view that man is inherently evil implies that people can never fully be trusted to behave in ways that will not pose a threat to themselves or others. The human organism has to be watched

*Man means mankind, humankind, the human race composed of *two* genders.

and restrained every step of the way, lest its true nature take over its tentative civilized one. In this context, values and moral codes of behavior must be hammered into people.

Graves also describes the humanistic and organismic view:

1. That man's nature is not a set thing, that it is ever emergent, that it is an open system, not a closed system.
2. That man's nature evolves by saccadic, quantum-like jumps from one steady system to another.
3. That man's values change from system to system as his total psychology emerges in new form with each quantum-like jump to a new steady state of being.

Does this view imply that anything goes? No, it suggests that the human organism strives to grow and attain its potential. The organism values its own life and recognizes that this same value operates in all human organisms. Values and moral codes of behavior become a matter of what is best for each person; each person can be trusted to know what is the most appropriate course of action. Values and morals are internally incorporated into the psychic core of the individual and the values and morals of others one trusts are considered.

A third view of the nature of man is described by psychologist Abraham Maslow (1971). He suggests that man is by nature essentially good or at least neutral; man is not inherently evil.

One's answer to the question, "How do I perceive the basic nature of man?" helps one understand one's own values and moral codes of behavior and those of others. Three suggested views see man as sinful and aggressive, neutral, or open and dynamic. This latter view implies that people can be trusted to behave in ways which are individually constructive and do not pose a direct threat to the physical well-being of others. It is obvious that the view one holds will ultimately decide how one will deal with values and moral codes of behavior; either by influence or imposition: either in an atmosphere of trust or one of suspicion.

DIFFERENT MORAL CODES AND VALUES

Of late there has been much discussion and conjecture about the generation gap and the communication gap. Adults usually hold one of two views concerning the moral codes and values of younger people. The first view takes the position that

Today, in the minds of many, there is a passionate certitude as to what is wrong with man. He is simply breaking apart at his moral seams. From every direction fingers point with certainty to the evidence that he is becoming ethically decrepit (Graves, p. 121).

Many adults are of the opinion that much of the behavior they observe in the young people of today is the result of moral deterioration. Young people are taught the worthy and valid morals and values which were embraced by preceding generations, but for some mysterious reason they seem to reject them. They have replaced them with codes which reflect an ethical breakdown.

A second view, in direct opposition to the view of moral decrepitness, suggests that

> The new morality is a more open and freer style of life than used to be known. The moral imperatives of previous generations which told people how to behave and what to believe under all situations are gone. We no longer accept hard and fast rules of conduct; instead, we develop our styles of life according to individual judgment and decision (Ferm, p. 38).

This position acknowledges that moral codes and values of today are different and new, but there is no evaluative negative connotation attached. Simply, many people have recently embraced values and moral codes of behavior which seem to reflect internal individual development rather than external imposition. This development process requires painstaking scrutinization of needs, goals, and objectives on the individual's part.

Many who adhere to the more traditional position that morals and values should be imposed tend to feel threatened by individuals who choose to carve out their own relevant and meaningful codes. This is certainly understandable. "Why would anyone go to all the trouble of questioning and evaluating morals and values when all one has to do is behave the way he/she is supposed to?" It is exactly these "supposed to's" that many people are rejecting. They want to know what is behind them; they seek explanations and reasons. "Why is a girl not supposed to call a boy on the phone and ask him for a date?" Many young people are not satisfied with the response "Well, nice girls don't do that. They just never have." Ferm (1968) suggests that "if we are to preserve some aspects of our older patterns of behavior, we must defend them on reasonable rather than authoritarian grounds (p. 38)." If our explanations rest on nothing but "this is how it always has been," then perhaps it is time to look carefully at the values or moral codes of behavior being questioned.

Ferm also suggests that if we respond to questioning about morals and values with "take it on faith," we're likely to convince the person posing the question that we're either being dishonest, have something to hide, or consider the question trivial. If, in response to a young person's questions such as "What is wrong with taking drugs?" or "Why shouldn't I have pre-marital sex?" the answering adult falls back on the use of *should's, should not's, supposed to's,* and *ought's,* chances are that the explanation is going to ring hollow.

Responses to such question should (I really tried not to use that word!) and must reflect that the adult did some homework. Facts, figures, statistics and research must be included plus open and honest statements such as "I really don't know," "It has been my experience that..." and "It is my opinion that...." It is through the use of these kinds of responses that the needs of the person questioning can be verbalized and dealt with.

Needs

Maslow views man as being motivated by basic needs and metaneeds. *Basic needs* are hunger, affection, security, and self-esteem. These are deficiency needs—requirements which are instinctive or inherent, which may result in the person's becoming sick if they are not fulfilled. They are hierarchical, meaning that one's hunger or physiological needs must be fulfilled before one can adequately think about fulfilling the need for affection. Likewise, one's needs for hunger and affection must be fulfilled before one can competently seek the fulfillment of security needs, and so on.

Metaneeds are growth needs. They include justice, goodness, beauty, order, and unity. These also are instinctive or inherent, but they are not hierarchical in arrangement as they are equally potent and can be fairly easily substituted for one another.

Viewing human needs in this way helps explain why ten minutes before supper is a futile time to try to explain to a young child who is cranky from hunger why he/she should be trying to get along with a sibling. Needs shift in priority; although an older child might accept that dinner is on its way and at the same time deal effectively with the sibling problem, younger children have not learned to deal with conflicting needs quite so successfully.

This is not to suggest that an awareness of needs is justification for unacceptable behavior; rather, it helps us to understand why children sometimes behave the ways in which they do. A parent might respond to the above situation by saying, "Hey, I can see that you are starving to death, but even so, I cannot tolerate your pummeling little brother. I want to suggest that you either come in the kitchen with me or go rest on your bed." This helps the child to understand that the adult acknowledges different needs while at the same time assists the child with suggestions for more acceptable behavior.

It is possible that the child in the example is in fact not hungry. The real need might be to keep the younger sibling out of his/her toys. At any rate, if the child feels that the adult is genuinely trying to appreciate his/her needs, the child can feel comfortable in responding "No. I am not hungry. I just want to keep so-and-so out of my things." The adult can then deal with that situation. Oftentimes adults observe behavior in children that they feel is contrary to the moral codes of behavior they would like to see developing; instead of trying to get at the children's needs, they deal only with the observable behavior. This is not particularly helpful to the child who is usually too resentful and frustrated to really listen to the adult.

An appreciation of needs is helpful to understanding our own values and codes of moral behavior and those of the people with whom we interact. If we can understand why a person perhaps behaves in a certain way, then we are in a more effective position for influencing related behavior. "I think I know why you did such and such and I would like to share with you some thoughts I have about that behavior."

SEQUENTIAL DEVELOPMENT OF MORAL BEHAVIOR

Psychologist Lawrence Kohlberg's model is helpful in understanding the relationship between morals and values and children. For twelve years Kohlberg and his colleagues studied the same group of seventy-five boys, following their development at three-year intervals from early adolescence through young manhood. At the start of the study the boys were aged ten to sixteen; at the conclusion, their ages ranged from twenty-two to twenty-eight years. Inspired by Jean Piaget's structural approach (discussed in Chapter 5), Kohlberg developed a typological scheme describing general structures and forms of moral thought which are identifiable independently of the specific content of given moral decisions and/or actions. The research suggests that the child has his/her own moralities or series of moralities which are sequential and hierarchical in development. These three moral levels and their related stages are highlighted.

1. Preconventional Level (approximately ages four to ten): The child links types of behavior with their consequences — good behavior means a reward; bad behavior means a punishment.

Stage 1: The child is oriented toward punishment and might is right. He/she unquestioningly accepts superior power.

Stage 2: The child is concerned with his/her own needs and occasionally with those of others. Fairness and equal sharing are defined in a physical and pragmatic way.

"The capacity of 'properly behaved' children at this age to engage in cruel behavior when there are holes in the power structure is sometimes noted as tragic *(Lord of the Flies, High Wind in Jamaica)*, (p. 26)." It seems that during this stage of moral development the child wants to see and feel the consequences of his/her behavior. Might is right and moral decisions seem to revolve around who has what power to wield and how this power can affect the child, especially physically.

2. Conventional Level (early and mid-teen years): The child's concern is with conforming to, maintaining, supporting, and justifying the social order.

Stage 3: Good behavior is defined in terms of its acceptance and approval by other people.

Stage 4: One earns respect by performing dutifully.

3. Postconventional Level (young adult and adult years): A person holds morals and values which he/she considers valid apart from social endorsement.

Stage 5: The person is concerned with general rights and makes allowances for personal values and opinions.

Stage 6: The person develops universal principles of justice, equality, and human rights, and a respect for the dignity of human beings.

To arrive at his levels and stages of moral development, Kohlberg presented the boys in the study with hypothetical moral dilemmas, all deliberately philosophical. By using this approach, he could determine each boy's stage of thought for each of the twenty-five basic moral concepts presented. For example, the six stages for the Value of Human Life are typologically presented as follows:

1. The value of human life is confused with the value of physical objects.

2. The value of human life is evaluated in terms of satisfying the needs of its possessor.

3. The value of human life is based on the empathy and affection of family members and others towards its possessor.

4. Life is viewed as being sacred in terms of its place in a categorical moral or religious order of rights and duties.

5. Life is valued both in terms of its relation to the welfare of the community and as its being a universal human right.

6. The value of human life is reflected as a universal respect for the individual.

These stages correspond to Kohlberg's six general stages described earlier. A similar scheme has been delineated for each of the other twenty-four basic moral concepts used in the study. Kohlberg suggests that stages are sequentially fixed, come one at a time, and are not skipped. After conducting experimental moral discussion classes with children, Kohlberg found that a child at an earlier stage of development tends to move on to the next stage when exposed to a child one stage further along, but not when exposed to a child who is more than one stage further along.

If moral development is sequential and hierarchical as suggested by Kohlberg's research, then it is easier to appreciate children's "mysterious" values and moral codes of behavior. Adults often conclude that children are being defiant and rebellious when they persist in behaving in the same unacceptable ways. It is possible that at such times children are in fact unable to understand and put into practice adult suggestions for acceptable behavior. The suggestions may simply be meaningless to them at their particular stage of moral development.

Kohlberg's work suggests that if a child is in, say, Stage 2, he/she is unable to incorporate Stage 4 behavior into his/her repertoire of responses until he/she has experienced Stage 3. This is not to say that as adults we are to sit idly by tolerating behavior that is unacceptable; we should share our feelings about the behavior with the child. But we should also be open to the possibility that the child truly cannot incorporate our suggestions into his/her behavior yet.

This helps explain why so many children really seem to have difficulty in accepting adult explanations about why they shouldn't hit younger children. The child is perhaps in a stage of moral development in which Might Is Right and finds it totally confusing and incomprehensible when an adult talks about other people's rights. This appreciation will develop in time, as will other morals and values. Meanwhile it might be very constructive for the adult to keep in mind the possibility that moral development is sequential and hierarchical in nature.

LABELING BEHAVIOR

Thus far the discussion of moral codes of behavior and values has emphasized the importance of trying to understand the needs of the behaver. Observed behavior is often judged according to the morals and values held by the observer; hence we use such terms as "right," "wrong," "good," and "bad." There is a tendency to extend the use of such terms to generalize the total person. An observer who finds a person's behavior "wrong" or "bad" on repeated occasions is prone to sum up that person's total worth as "bad." There is a danger, especially when children are involved, for this judgment to turn into a self-fulfilling prophecy. The child senses "You are a bad person" enough times and concludes, "Yeah, I guess it is true. I am a bad person."

It is obvious that such a belief about oneself has the potential to incapacitate the individual for further growth. "What's the use of trying? I am a bad person. No good person would want anything to do with me." Many times this attitude is manifested by a child's shunning other people or being afraid to show any independent behavior before checking it out with adults. Such a child begins many questions with the phrase "Should I . . .?"

Rather than indicating a close, sharing adult/child relationship, such questions may mean that the child is dependent upon the adult for moral and value decisions. A child does need guidance and support on such matters, but all too often, well-intentioned adults try to solve the whole problem. This approach suggests that there is only one answer to moral issues. It by-passes a very necessary consideration of needs. Further, it suggests that adults are the only ones who can really answer questions related to morals and values.

Kohlberg cites research (Hartshone and May, 1930) in which it was found that

> regarding honesty, for instance . . . almost everyone cheats some of
> the time, and that if a person cheats in one situation, it doesn't
> mean that he will or won't in another. In other words, it is not an
> identifiable character trait, dishonesty, that makes a child cheat in
> a given situation (Kohlberg, p. 27).

It is unfortunate that I did not have access to this kind of thinking when I was teaching elementary school. I remember many incidents that went something like this: Kenny would steal someone's pencil and then deny the theft with admirable steadfastness until an eye-witness would call his bluff. Based on that one incident I would conclude that "Kenny is a dishonest person." I now know that this feeling on my part determined the kind of relationship we had for the rest of the year.

I fell into the trap of assuming how Kenny would behave in all situations based on his behavior in one isolated situation. Kenny would ask to go to the library by himself and I would not let him go because in my mind he was a dishonest boy; I knew what a dishonest boy would do at the library without me there to supervise. If he stole pencils, he was certainly capable of stealing books! I arranged things so Kenny could remain nothing but dishonest in my mind. I never allowed him the opportunity to act in independent and honest ways and I am sure Kenny sensed this. I made him pay for stealing a pencil for the rest of the school year; I can only wonder what the long-range effects of my interactions have been.

I am not suggesting that one need not be concerned with the consequences of behavior. Quite the contrary, consequences are of the utmost importance, but the point is that I never even considered Kenny's need for stealing that pencil and I never did anything constructive to help him deal with the incident. My only contribution was punishment. Kenny is not a unique child in my teaching past; I have made the same mistake with many children. It is with a heavy heart that I think about all the Kennys in my life.

Recently I experienced another theft by children but I came away from the incident with good feelings. While at home I noticed that about half of the vitamins in Heather's jar were missing. I shrugged it off thinking I had just lost track of what was in the jar. Later that afternoon one of my neighbors told me that she had overheard a couple of kids talking about their hidden cache of vitamin pills and she thought she heard my name mentioned somewhere in the conversation. My initial thought was, "Those beastly little kids stole some vitamin pills." I remember my imagination going wild with such thoughts as "Check the piggy banks. Got to keep the house locked up. Can't let any of the kids in when I'm not home." And on and on. Mentally I had all but sent the entire neighborhood to a reform school. Also, I was condemning the kids' parents wondering how they had so successfully raised such sneaky and devious children. Fortunately something inside of me said, "Whoa, Karen" and I thought of all the Kennys I had known.

Later that afternoon about ten of the group were playing in Heather's room; I casually strolled in and announced, "I need to talk with you all." I proceeded to tell them that I had noticed some of Heather's vitamin pills missing and that this really worried me for a couple of reasons. I discussed my concern about anyone taking any kind of medicine that had not been prescribed for them by either a doctor or their parents, and I talked about how uneasy it made me feel to think that things could disappear from our home. I told them how important it was for me to feel that I could trust each and every one of them; how I needed to be assured that we all thought enough of each other that they could come and go in our home when we were not there.

One of their first concerns was, "Do you know who did it?" They sure as hell all knew! My two culprits were looking down at their feet, sort of spellbound, with the rest of the group staring at them. I told them that my concern was not with who did it but with the consequences of that kind of behavior. Their next concern was whether or not they could still come and go in the house. I assured them that they could because I felt confident that we could all work the whole thing through. I left the room and I could hear them all whispering about something.

A few minutes later the two little girls whom I suspected were following me around. Everywhere I turned, there they were. Finally I told them that it looked as if they wanted to talk with me. They fidgeted, shuffled their feet, and bobbed their heads from side to side. Finally they said no, they didn't have anything special to talk about so I said, "Well, let's carry on." A few days later one of them mentioned to me that she could see Heather's cough medicine on top of the dresser and that I would probably want to put it in a safer place. Well, yes, I did. Thank you very much.

CONSEQUENCES OF BEHAVIOR

The relationship between moral decisions and their consequences must be considered. Judith and Donald Smith (1968) point out that the consequences of behavior can be viewed as being *immediate* or *delayed*. Children learn quite readily to anticipate immediate consequences, but the concept of delayed consequences is difficult to grasp, even for adults. A child who swipes a candy bar from the local store can appreciate the immediate consequences. He/she must experience the hassle of returning it to the store or paying for it, probably while feeling, "I am bad." If this happens on a Monday, all concerned, especially the child, would like to think that it is a closed issue by Tuesday morning. However, come Friday the child returns to the store only to be told by the owner that he/she is not allowed in the store anymore.

These are the delayed consequences. They are usually unanticipated and harsh, and often extend well into the future. Even though children can usually grasp immediate consequences, they need added guidance in discerning delayed ones. Adults can be most helpful in this area by pointing out some "What if's" and "Have you considered's?" These are most effective at the time a child is confronted with a moral decision, but even in retrospect, that is, after the child has made a decision and is confronted by the consequences, they can help him/her realize the wide range of possible consequences. This kind of experience helps a child learn to pinpoint and weigh alternatives.

Children also need help in recognizing how their behavior can affect the people with whom they interact, especially those with whom they have close relationships. Children and adults alike want to feel that their moral decisions affect only themselves, but this is unrealistic. A child who decides to take back all the wood he/she has donated to the building of the neighborhood clubhouse needs to be aware that even though it is his/her wood, reclaiming it can have an affect on his/her relationships with the other children involved. This is not to say that the child should or should not retrieve the wood. That decision is the child's.

The point is that many times we behave in ways which we truly believe do not affect other people, but which ultimately do; we need to help children be aware of this fact of life.

> Our task then is to train children to be moral by training them how to make decisions. For whatever else morality may be, it at least includes making wise decisions (Smith and Smith, p. 90).

An important part of making wise decisions includes having access to as much information as possible, and oftentimes children need adult assistance in gathering these data.

THE ACQUISITION OF MORALS AND VALUES

In the above quotation there is a reference to *training* children to make moral decisions. I think the use of this word requires exploration. Many adults tend to think that morals and values can be treated as a commodity which is wrapped, sealed with a bow and presented to children. This suggests an external imposition which is likely to be rejected if the contents of the package do not happen to coincide with the child's needs and goals. It seems that many adults do not recognize that the acquisition of morals and values is so subtle and gradual that it is difficult to pinpoint the exact time at which a child learns specific behaviors that are morally acceptable or unacceptable. Values and morals are learned more through a continuous process of osmosis than by direct teaching.

Modeling is frequently used. The child observes the behavior of others and hears their opinions and ideas. Obviously, actual behavior and verbal statements are not always synonymous. Research suggests that children will base decisions on behavior they have observed rather than on things they have heard. In the long run, "Do as I do" is the most effective and lasting advice. For instance, a lecture on sharing can be rejected by a child; but if this same child observes adults sharing with neighbors, friends, and other children, he/she is more apt to behave the same.

Live your morals and values. This seems so obvious, yet many adults rely on sermonizing, moralizing, and lecturing. What does this mean? Could it be that many adults recognize the disparity between their ideals and their actions and hope their children will only pick up their verbalizations? Does it mean that many adults are torn between the *should* syndrome and some of their own true feelings and beliefs? Adults who feel it necessary to explain and/or apologize for their behavior to children are not being completely open and honest with either themselves or their children. Children have an uncanny ability to pick up on such discrepancies.

Can adults transmit their most cherished values to their children? Gordon's answer (1970) is: "Of course—not only *can* you teach your values, but inevitably you *will* (p. 272)." But which ones will be transmitted? The ones which are an integrated part of an adult, or the ones the adult would like to see transmitted? The two are not always the same, and again it is emphasized that values which are lived are more likely to be transmitted.

However, "There are many behaviors of children that parents simply may not be able to change. The only alternative is to accept this (Gordon, p. 278)." This is a cold and hard fact. Many times adult values will not be accepted by children; then the adult must answer this question: "Can I still accept a child who rejects any of my values?"

5

"I don't mind if the kids play hide 'n go seek in my house."

"I'm afraid they'll break something. And besides, if they are allowed to play it in your house, they'll expect to play it in my house, too."

"Really, it's okay with me."

"Yeah but, children need

To Know Their Limitations

IN TERMS OF "Yeah but...," there appears to be a subtle implication that adults know their limitations and that children need to have theirs defined by adults. It is more realistic, rather, to think about limitations as phenomena which all people, regardless of age, need to be aware of in each of their one-to-one relationships. A husband has the right to know when his behavior causes anxiety and frustration in his wife, a wife needs the same kind of information from her husband, and children need to know when their behavior is offensive or unacceptable to other children and adults.

Many adults tend to view *knowing* limitations as simply a matter of telling another person what he/she may and may not do; this writer is suggesting that the process is actually twofold. First, one needs to know what behavior is unacceptable to another and *why*; second, one must recognize that limitations involve consequences. "If you persist in such and such behavior, you may expect me to do such and such." The distinction is subtle, but it is there. Many times adults disguise control and power under the umbrella "Children need to know their limitations." This is really merely an extension of authority and discipline. What adults are doing many times is in fact controlling children's behavior.

Of course children need to know their limitations, just as adults need to know theirs. Any person involved in a relationship has to know when his/her behavior is causing another person a problem. The word "limitations" in this context refers to behavior which is somehow straining or negatively affecting the relationship. It is not being used in a punitive way, which is its more common usage. After the unacceptable behavior is defined, "It really upsets me when you play kickball in the street, " the recipient has to know the *because* part of the feeling, "Because I am so afraid that you will be hurt by a car."

Gordon (1970) talks about these kinds of behavior in terms of the concrete and tangible impacts on the person who finds another's behavior unacceptable: "I care about you so much that it would just be more than I could bear if you were to get hurt and have to be hospitalized. It also worries me because hospitalization is so expensive." The caring part or fear of someone's getting hurt is definitely a real feeling but this in and of itself does not relay the tangible and concrete effects of the other's behavior. The part about the expense of hospitalization does in fact define the effects. Many a reader might conclude that moving from a fear of injury to dollars and cents is crude and callous, but this approach, which states limitations in terms of the relationship and tangible effects, has a much better chance of being accepted by the other person; he/she can appreciate and accept the impacts on the other person.

This is not the same as saying to another person: "If you persist in playing kickball in the street you will have to go to your room for the afternoon." Even though the underlying feelings might be identical, (fear of injury from traffic), the message is different; it exudes controls and threats which are apt to make the recipient angry and defensive. Limitations are spelled out in this example, but in a punitive and negative way. The behavioral choices available to the recipient are different. When concrete and tangible effects are stated, the person behaving in the unacceptable way can ask himself/herself, "Do I accept that my behavior does in fact affect the other person?"

If it does, the person can go through the mental process: "Hey, I also care so much about the other person and our relationship that my behaving in such and such a way is just not all that important. Let's play kickball somewhere else rather than cause such great worry."

In this example it is also possible that the caring element is minimal: "So go worry, you old creep!" This, of course, reflects a deteriorated relationship. Such relationships exist, sometimes beyond reparation. It is incredibly painful to know that someone we care about doesn't give a damn about us. Some relationships can be salvaged and re-established on a foundation of trust and concern, but the cold hard fact is that many relationships are forever lost to us. How one uses the concept of limitations can have a vital impact on the stability and bond of our relationships.

When a person is told, "You can expect such and such from me if you continue to behave in such and such a way," all in the name of defining limitations, the recipient has different behavioral options available. He/she can take the attitude "Oh, all right, I won't play in the dumb street," or he/she can persist in the behavior and pay the price. Additionally, he/she can continue the behavior in devious ways where the object becomes one of not getting caught. In any case, the relationship suffers, through pent up resentment, having to endure a punishment, or guilt feelings for sneaking around. None of the options is particularly attractive and negative feelings between both parties are inevitable.

When one attempts to talk about another person's unacceptable behavior in concrete and tangible terms, some interesting and significant things become evident. "I cannot accept your being pals with So and So" is an example of offensive behavior. Why? "Because he/she is such a bum and you'll get a bad reputation; because I look bad having a child of mine hanging around with such a person; because you might pick up some bad habits from him/her." When one thinks about tangible and concrete effects it becomes evident that many times the *because* is hollow; in reality the reasons refer to morals and values and these are personal and individual matters. "It's *your* problem if you look bad because I hang around with So and So. " "Hey, it's *my* problem if I get a bad reputation or if I pick up bad habits."

In cases such as these, people often have difficulty stating how another's behavior has concrete and tangible effects on them— simply because it doesn't. Even though we often fight hard to convince ourselves and others that it does, the behavior is actually in the realm of morals and values.

Adults expend much unnecessary time and effort in defining limitations. They often use the definition of limitations to control and manipulate children's behavior. Granted, there are times when children require adult participation and consultation in defining limitations or in being made aware of behaviors that are unacceptable. But for the most part adults get entirely too involved in facets of this process that are unnecessary and even destructive to the adult-child relationships, especially when they try to incorporate the concept of concrete and tangible effects into these definitions of limitations.

Another related area which adults, and especially parents, must think about is how limitations are often decreed in such a way as to be absolute. Limitations are frequently handled as if they must apply to all relationships even though they were originally the result of only one given relationship. For example, when the neighborhood gang is playing I often ask if anyone wants to snack with Heather. Sometimes all the kids eat; at other times only a few of them nibble. If there is a child who has been told, "You will not eat between meals," I am unaware of it; all the kids have snacked with us at one time or another. However, if one of the kids has been told not to eat between meals, it must be a very disturbing feeling for that child to know that he/she could get caught at any moment with a mouthful of carrot by a disapproving parent.

It is a heavy and unnecessary burden for a child to have to bring to all relationships the limitations of his/her parental relationship. I have my own relationship with each of these children and I like to think that both the child and his/her parents trust me to be aware of the approaching dinner hour. Children enter into a variety of relationships with other adults; it should be a source of growth for a child to carve out and work through a different relationship with each individual adult. This process might well involve different limitations while that adult and child are interacting.

I will not eat dinner with any baby, our own included, on my lap. It just ruins my meal to have a kid squirming all over me picking through and fingering the food on my plate. This interferes with my appetite and I know from experience that it can lead to indigestion. I explained this to Heather a few times, and she has gotten the message that my particular lap is off limits during dinner. However, she knows which laps are available to her and under which conditions. My sister Janet would put aside a four pound lobster to have Heather sit on her lap during a meal and Heather knows this. Heather also realizes that Gramma's lap is off limits during the main course of the meal but on limits during dessert.

I used to think that I had to mandate some rule like "Heather is not allowed to play musical laps during the meal," but now I feel that these kinds of behavior are between Heather and the people with whom she interacts. People who know us no longer say, "Is it okay if we let Heather do such and such?" My typical response, which has almost become a joke, is, "That's between you and Heather." I really have enjoyed giving up the watchdog role and I feel that Heather is learning that the acceptability or unacceptability of much of her behavior only takes on meaning within the framework of her individual relationships with others. This also gives her a firsthand opportunity to learn that some behaviors such as biting and hitting, are not acceptable to anyone.

I have also found that this relinquishing of the watchdog role extends to friends' homes. Heather knows that when she is in Linda's home she may play with all the knick-knacks on her coffee table, but when she is in Jo's house, touching anything on her coffee table is off limits. Jo and Linda have worked this out with Heather; I don't have to play the role of the intermediary in such situations. I don't have to get a run down on limitations and make sure Heather carries them out. I don't have to get bogged down in the "Maybe you shouldn't touch that, Heather. Linda/Jo might not like it." Many a parent knows what a drag this can be and it often makes one wish they had never visited in the first place.

I do not have to second guess anyone on what is acceptable or unacceptable behavior for Heather. It is her behavior, she is responsible for it, and it really doesn't affect me. It is between Heather and Linda and Jo. I suspect that many parents would feel uncomfortable with this arrangement, but with family and good friends, I have found it both realistic and satisfying and I don't suffer pangs of guilt that I am expecting others to assume the responsibility of our child. Quite the contrary. I feel that by allowing Heather to work out relationships with the people in her life, I am behaving most responsibly. I might also add that on occasion Jo has put Heather out her back door because she felt that Heather was behaving irresponsibly in her home. That's okay with me. Not my problem. That's between Heather and Jo.

"Yeah but, children need to know their limitations." Most assuredly. Children need to know their limitations just as adults need to know theirs. Everyone has a right to be informed when his/her behavior causes a problem for another person. This person must ponder such questions as: Does this problem really have tangible effects on me or am I attempting to control and manipulate another's behavior? Am I trying to limit behavior by defining its effect on a relationship or am I perhaps using limits interchangeably with power and control?

KNOWING CHILDREN'S LIMITATIONS

Thus far this discussion has focused on limitations in a behavioral context. Adults also need an awareness of children's limitations as they grow and develop intellectually or cognitively. Intellectual activities, such as perceiving, thinking, abstracting, generalizing, and remembering, are not confined exclusively to cognitive processes but overlap into emotional processes. In short, cognitive and emotional (or affective) processes cannot be approached as separate and isolated. They are intertwined and ultimately affect human interactions and relationships. Adults need to be familiar with children's cognitive and emotional limitations. In this sense limitations refer to *capabilities*.

The work of Jean Piaget has been monumental in describing children's cognitive growth and development. Piaget was born in Switzerland in 1896 and is still totally involved in his work and research. His early works were translated into English in the 1920s and were followed by much criticism because he had studied a small number of subjects and his work lacked statistical verification and validation. Piaget was not initially concerned with methods of scientific research and most critics were not open to his ideas and suggestions. But in the 1950s, there was new interest in his work and since then his research has been replicated and validated. Piaget's ideas are now studied and considered to be extremely important.

Piaget's first sample was small indeed! He and his wife kept careful and detailed notes on the cognitive growth of their three children. From these early observations emerged Piaget's books on intellectual development during a child's first years of life. Piaget's other contributions include studies on childhood and adolescence, the development of the processes required to work with logical and mathematical concepts, and the development of perception. His research is brilliantly comprehensive and extensive, and there are many implications in Piaget's work for human relationships, especially adult-child interactions.

Piaget's basic construct is that there are formulated and sequential developmental stages of cognitive growth in children. He suggests that there are four categories through which every child must pass as he/she develops cognitively, but there are no fixed time durations. In other words, one stage must precede the next, but environmental factors can retard or accelerate movement through the stages. Consequently, the suggested ages for each stage are approximations.

Sensory-Motor Stage (birth to two years). During this stage the child learns about his/her muscles through extensive trial-and-error movements involving bodily control and eye-hand coordination. The child is also aware of his/her senses. Using both muscles and senses the child develops certain habits for dealing with external objects in the environment. The sensory-motor stage is so named because the infant's earliest manifestations of intelligence form and are observable through personal sensory perceptions and motor activities. The child follows a moving object, turns in response to a noise, and grabs and touches things. During this stage the child is compelled to manipulate objects in the environment and is not being consciously rebellious in going after things that "he/she knows better than to touch." The child's natural and innate curiosity drives him/her to explore objects.

Many adults feel that even at this young age children should be made not to touch certain objects, and that with enough "NO! NO's!" the child can learn that he/she must suffer the consequences of disapproval for continuing this behavior. It must be understood that this situation is very confusing for such young children. They have a genuine need to touch the objects in their environment and they also have a genuine need to be accepted and approved by the significant adults in their lives. Older children are able to cognitively respond to "I do not want you to touch this because..." but the younger child simply lacks the language and experience to comprehend this concept.

The parent who removes precious objects from the environment is not being overindulgent and permissive and is not giving the child free reign over the home. In child-proofing a child's environment for the first couple years of life, parents recognize his/her developmental limitations. It is a way of saying, "I recognize your need to explore the things in your environment. I also recognize your need not to be constantly nagged by me about touching certain things as this can put you in conflict with your natural inclinations and make you feel guilty. I can help you resolve this conflict by removing certain things from your surroundings. When you get a little older you will not want to touch my things and you won't because by then you will care about me and will be able, even in your own awkward way, to appreciate my needs. I remove these objects for the present happily because I know I am encouraging your growth.''

There will be, obviously, some taboo objects in the environment which cannot be removed; if these are few in number a child can readily accept occasional "No! No's!" All too often it seems that many parents almost purposely overstock the environment with taboo objects just so they can work out their own need to show the child who's boss. As suggested earlier, the child already knows who the "boss" is; emphasizing this type of obedience can be destructive to the relationship.

It is during this stage of cognitive growth and development that the child begins to learn about object constancy or permanence. Initially persons or objects exist in the child's life only when he/she can see them. After the first few months the child begins to realize that many people and objects leave or are gone temporarily, but that they can be counted on to return or reappear. This concept of permanence can be startling for a child. Trusting children do not seem to have as much difficulty with their parents' absence as do less trusting children. Children who are not exposed to a wide variety of adults and children in their early months tend to be more suspicious of their parents' departures when they get older. They develop too much dependency on them.

Many adults, knowingly or unknowingly, foster this dependency by not allowing their babies opportunity to interact with others alone, without the parent being present. The subtle message is, "I am the only one who can really take care of you." The child often senses this protection and it is reflected in fears of "What will happen to me if mom and dad leave me with someone else?" A baby, by phylogenetic design, is dependent on adults as are the young of no other species of organism, but many adults inculcate an emotional dependency that is detrimental to the child's growth. If parents distrust people, their child learns to do the same. Not yet fully understanding object constancy or permanence, the child can come to overtrust his/her parents to the point of dependency if not given the opportunity to interact with a variety of people. Parents should ponder their own needs for having dependent children.

During this stage of cognitive growth, the child learns the rudiments of causality, time, and space. "What will happen if...?" becomes an important activity and includes such irritating and disconcerting behavior as the dropping, throwing, and mixing of things. Every parent has lived through or can look forward to a child intentionally dropping dishes and objects and attempting to do it over and over again, objects being swished around the toilet bowl, trash being strewn all over, smushing of food on the highchair tray, flower pots being overturned, drawers being emptied, rolls of toilet paper being unfurled and dragged all over the house. These types of behavior are innate inclinations and they do not describe a naughty child who is trying to be defiant or belligerent. The behaviors are not a child's way of pleading for discipline or limitations. They are merely experiments with "What will happen if...?" as the child tries to make some sense out of his/her environment. Appreciating this can make it more bearable for adults as they cope with the incredibly frustrating messes their children have left in their wakes.

Modifying the environment is the most viable alternative for children of this age group. Drawers can be tied shut, bathroom doors closed, (rest assured, you will know immediately that one time in a million when the bathroom door is left open!), newspaper can be spread under the highchair. Many people feel that going to all this bother is nonsense and it is easier to just go the "No! No!" route. It may be more expedient and less time-consuming for the parents to follow the child around saying "No you can't do this" and "No you can't do that," but oftentimes this approach results in overly timid and fearful toddlers who live with with their heads crooked back at a 45-degree angle anticipating another "No, No, No."

Some children decide it isn't worth the crook in the neck and just evolve into passive beings who are afraid to try new activities and experiences. The possibility exists that such a channeling of a child's natural energies and interest, even though initially easier for parents, could translate to the child as "I really don't care what you think and feel you need to do. I will tell you how to behave."

In short, the sensory-motor stage is a time during which a child's main concerns are related to muscular and sensory development. Later, as the child learns to represent objects and people by word or gesture, he/she begins to know about things that exist beyond immediate sight and touch.

Preoperational Stage (about two to seven years). During this stage of intellectual growth the child learns to use symbolic substitutes such as mental images and language. Single words, usually nouns, are learned at a rapid rate, followed by two-word phrases usually including a verb to represent an internalization of action related to the noun. From the nouns "Mommy" and "Daddy" the child moves into attaching action thoughts such as "Mommy away," or "Daddy do it." Interestingly enough, linguist Dan Slobin (1972) has found that children first use one word communication, then two words, then three words, and finally at this point are able to communicate in complete sentences.

This developmental approach to the spoken language is universal and Slobin further suggests that the child unconsciously tries to express himself/herself in complete thoughts and sentences without any conscious attempt at deciphering grammatical structure. A young child who barks in a general's voice, "Mommy go away" is not attempting to be disrespectful or aggressive in the sense of assuming control of a relationship. Rather, the child is so involved with the acquisition of language, so totally delighted with using words and observing reactions, and so immersed in structuring reality that it only appears that he/she is being aggressive. At this point many adults panic and assume that if they do not straighten the kid out, they will be saddled with a potentially demanding and pushy child.

Adults can help children learn the fine shading of communication, how tone and presentation may not always be in concert with what a child is really feeling. "When you say 'Mommy go away' like that, it sounds like you are really mad at me and it hurts my feelings. Do you mean 'Mommy go away' (said with anger) or do you mean 'Mommy go away' (said with gentleness)?" Even a young child can respond to this kind of approach—perhaps not effectively initially, but if used consistently there will come a time when the child can respond to it. This helps him/her learn that the adult recognizes how exciting it is to master language while at the same time it helps to develop the awareness that the way in which words are spoken is also a part of communication.

We have already discussed the terrible two's as being a mythical stage. Often the most terrible thing a child has to deal with is the expectation by adults that he/she will behave terribly. This attitude is sometimes self-fulfilling since the child is sensitive to adult feelings of "Oh, I just knew this would happen. This child is behaving this way because he/she has reached the terrible two's. This stage is just as horrendous as everyone said it would be."

Consequently, many adults get so bogged down in expecting terrible behavior that they often react to innocent situations as if they were situations of rebellion and defiance. After a while a child may just get the idea that defiance is expected. Children are not oblivious or uncomprehending when they repeatedly hear their parents say to other adults, "So and So is just driving me bananas. Into the terrible two's, you know." Much of a child's behavior is frustrating to adults, but if adults are aware of a child's cognitive and affective limitations, then they will be less apt to conclude that the child is intentionally trying to frustrate others. The frustration is with the child who is bombarded with the realization that he/she has feelings which can be communicated via language and that this communication can cause reactions in people.

The terrible two's is not an inevitable stage of growth and development. It is a difficult time, but with adults understanding the numerous and complex processes taking place within children, much of the difficulty can be alleviated for both.

One of my friends told me that she always felt guilty that her own three children never went through the terrible two's. She had heard about this stage, waited for it with ghoul-like anticipation, and when it just never materialized, she felt that she had done something wrong and somehow deprived her children of a necessary stage. Further examination of her relationships with her children suggested that she had always made an effort to be aware of their needs as well as her own and that she had always interacted with them by asking herself, "What is really going on inside of these kids?" This effort resulted in open, honest, and trusting relationships between this mother and her three children. Jo no longer feels guilty that her children did not develop and react "according to the book" and she now takes great pride in her relationships with her children.

The preoperational stage is a time of heightened fantasy and make-believe. Fantasy gives a child safe and unthreatening ways to release emotions and feelings that are confusing and at times frightening, allowing him/her to possess some control over the environment. Role-playing is serious and vital work for children, and by observing role-playing situations, adults can gain firsthand knowledge of their children's perceptions about other children and adults. Playing house is a favorite, as family life is a common experience. Children at this age can be counted on to mirror the kinds of relationships they feel they have with special adults. Mothers and fathers who scream and yell at their children can observe these same children playing screaming and yelling mommies and daddies. Gentle and considerate mothers and fathers can observe their children playing gentle and considerate parents.

The accompanying dialogue is also fascinating and enlightening. "I don't want you to be the mother. You always holler. Let Lee be the mother. She's a nice mommy." The nice mommy says, as they play house, "We need to talk about such and such." The hollering mommy says, "Go to your room. And you don't get any supper." (While all this is going on I must keep my face glued to my book lest I lose my non-identity. It seems as if the role-players assume that if Karen is holding a book, she must be reading and not listening to them. If I put the book down, the action stops or is moved to Heather's room behind closed doors. It is a tricky business for an adult to observe such role-playing!)

Fantasies are necessary for the preoperational child and must be accepted by adults as being serious and real for the child. It is detrimental to ridicule a child's fantasies. "Oh you silly thing, why would you talk to a friend or animal who doesn't even exist?" degrades a very real part of a child's existence. An adult can acknowledge a child's fantasy as being fantasy while at the same time relaying an attitude of serious acceptance. "I see that you're talking to your imaginary elephant. Seems like you really enjoy talking with him." The child is able to react, "We both know my elephant is not really real, and yes, I sure do like talking to him." Actually, a child's fantasy world is a private domain, but occasionally adults are invited to enter it. "Mom, can we set a place at the table for Herman?" (Herman, of course, is an imaginary gazelle.) "Sure we can set a place for Herman. Sometime I really would like to hear about Herman if you wanted to talk about him. He is yours and only yours and he sure seems important to you. I think it would be fun to have you talk about him,"—an accepting and non-threatening response.

Modeling and imitation are used extensively by the preoperational child. Children interact with other people and often state a desire to be "just like Mr. Jones when I grow up." Oftentimes children get so into imitating behaviors that they will talk like, sit like and in general, be like the person they adore. Children in this stage usually have difficulty in describing the reasons for their adoration and are inclined to sum it up as "because Mr. Jones is nice." Other times children will model their behavior after people they don't really know on a personal level, such as a television star or entertainer. All such activities are serious business and it is devastating to the child to be told that he/she could really never be like Donny Osmond or Billie Jean King.

Rather than ridiculing children's idols, adults can help children focus in on those attributes or characteristics that appeal to them. "So you say you would like to be just like your school principal or your science teacher when you grow up. Can you figure out why you like them so much?" By respecting children's fantasies and acknowledging their importance in helping children structure life, adults can learn all kinds of things about their children and, indirectly, about themselves.

Many adults fear that if they do not remind children that fantasies and make-believe are not real, children will not be able to distinguish between reality and the imaginary. Children know when they are indulging in make-believe. They just need to be assured that it is an okay activity and that they are entitled to fantasize about hopes, dreams, and aspirations. Adults do it. If a child prefers to spend a majority of his/her time in a self-constructed world of make-believe, it might be well for adults to examine the child's real world which, for most children, tends to be complex and confusing. Fantasies give a child an opportunity to look at isolated bits and pieces of the real world over which he/she can maintain control, thereby starting to deal with the complexity and confusion of reality.

The preoperational stage is a period of tremendous language growth. Through the use of language and mental images the child learns to represent both the outside world and his/her inner world of emotions and feelings. For two- to four-year-old children, heard words are usually associated with objects, and concept formation grows out of re-occurring experiences. The four- to seven-year-old child begins dealing with an intuitive use of concepts. Direct perceptual comparisons tend to be accurate, (Which is bigger? Which is fatter?), but associated concepts tend to be confused. Complex situations are seen as wholes which defy analysis and conclusions are based on superficial impressions. "This must be a short and easy book to read because it is thin."

Many times children are given tasks to do which are simply beyond their capabilities—not within the realm of their cognitive limitations. For example, adults often give children tasks to do such as "Take this tape and put it in the desk drawer which is the second from the bottom on the right." Oftentimes children simply do not understand the task. It is beyond their grasp of spacial and directional comprehension. **Rather than saying, "I am too stupid to understand what you have just said,"** they react with "I don't want to do it." Adults tend to assume that they have a behavioral or discipline problem to deal with when in reality, they are confronted by a cognitive difficulty, disguised in the behavior. Such a situation may result in hassling. This is unfortunate, as the problem could be alleviated by a step-by-step breakdown of the task so that the child could follow through on it. The child really would like to do what is requested but simply cannot when he/she is asked to deal with intellectual skills which have not yet been acquired.

Period of Concrete Operations (about seven to eleven years). In discussing Piaget's work, psychologist Mary Ann Pulaski (1971) defines the term "concrete operations" as meaning that the child "can operate in thought on concrete objects or their representations. He can serialize, extend, subdivide, differentiate, or combine existing structures into new relationships or groupings. He can now think logically about things rather than accepting surface appearances (p. 26)." A child in this stage can compare the size of print in two books and base a personal conclusion on which would be shorter to read on more than just superficial appearances. Such a child can compare the length of one book with another even though the actual books are not held in his/her hands. Operations can be imagined and results can be anticipated. Where the preoperational child asks a maddening number of "Why?" questions a child in this stage will experiment with "What if...?" It is very common for children in this stage of intellectual growth to question rules, regulations, theories, and ideas that are presented to them. They are not necessarily being wiseguys; they are using their developing abilities to imagine and anticipate the possible outcomes when situations are manipulated.

Children in the concrete stage can distinguish such associated concepts like $4 + 1 = 5$, $1 + 4 = 5$, $5 - 4 = 1$, $5 - 1 = 4$. It is difficult for a child in this stage to operate mentally on such a mathematical concept, and most children develop the concept only after working it through on a concrete level, such as by using an abacus. Children in this stage have more experience structuring their reality and they are less likely to unquestioningly accept adults' ideas. They are not rejecting adults' views and opinions to be nasty and defiant; rather, they are using their abilities to recognize the many facets of a situation or idea and are trying to reconcile all these parts into a whole. They think at deeper, more sophisticated, and more perceptive levels than in earlier stages.

Period of Formal Operations (about eleven or twelve years on). It is during this period of intellectual growth that the child can deal with hypotheses and can logically project what possibilities might follow in a given sequence. He/she is able to follow forms of reasoning and during this stage mathematical models become meaningful. Operations involving symbols or abstract ideas can be carried out in the mind and the child does not need concrete representations of objects to deal with them mentally. Relationships involving more than one variable can be considered and comprehended and accurate comparisons can be made deductively.

In summary, Piaget's theory of cognitive growth and development characterizes intelligence as an adaptive process. This development of intellectual capacity passes through the four described stages, always in the order presented above. The rate at which an individual moves from one stage to another varies with the individual and his/her particular social environment. The theory maintains that we learn by doing and by interacting with our environment. Many adults assume that conceptualization precedes verbalization. This is not always true. Because a child can speak eloquently about something, be it the Commutative Law of Addition or the evils of alcohol, this is no guarantee that the child has conceptualized or internalized this verbiage. The lecturing used by so many adults to teach children is often ineffective. Children hear the words, but many times, due to their cognitive limitations, they are unable to assimilate them into meaningful and applicable structures.

It is imperative that adults be aware of children's intellectual limitations. This awareness will enable adults to get behind observable behavior and to consider the true motivations governing it. "Is the child able to understand what I have just said?" "Am I asking something of that child which at present is beyond his/her capabilities?" Adults need to be aware of children's limitations.

6
Yeah But, Now What?

THE PRECEDING chapters have focused on some of the fundamental issues we face when interacting with children. Questions have been raised, theories have been considered. We must now lessen the gap between thinking about these ideas and actually implementing them.

Our primary concern so far has been with the *what* aspect or with the *content* involved in adult-child interactions. But to remain with theory is static. To move from theory to action requires a consideration of the *how* , or of *process* . How might adults go about interacting with children in the most constructive ways? This entails changing the more traditional approaches one previously used. Change is a process. "Yeah but, children need authority, discipline, morals and values, and to know their limitations." Yeah but, now what?

Most of our relationships tend to be content-oriented. Our primary concern is *what* is said in our interactions, *what* behaviors we observe, and *what* behaviors we hope to observe. Very little assistance is offered in helping adults to back up, to get in touch with the motivating forces behind observable behavior. Without an appreciation and understanding of this technique, our interactions tend to be haphazard and unpredictable.

I have chosen the concept of curiosity to act as a vehicle for describing some of the subtle but important differences between content and process.

USING THE PHENOMENON OF CURIOSITY TO UNDERSTAND CONTENT

In a historical sense, the phenomenon of curiosity has proven to be a definite boon to civilization; all the inventions and discoveries through the ages have been the result of someone's driving desire To Know. In fact, the eminent Behaviorist psychologist B. F. Skinner even goes so far as to suggest that the desire to know has perpetuated the species.

> There can be no doubt of the survival value of the inquiring spirit—of curiosity, of exploration, of the need to dominate the media, of the urge to control the forces of nature. The world will never be wholly known, and man can't help trying to know more and more of it (Skinner, p. 126).

Exactly what is this mysterious, powerful, illusive thing we call Curiosity? One psychologist defines it as "the urge to investigate the environment, particularly when it is novel or unusual; a general drive which includes or overlaps with the exploratory drive and the manipulative drive (Goldenson, p. 284)." Only a few decades ago most psychologists assumed that an organism investigates its environment only if motivated by such physiological needs as hunger or sex.

The work of Romanes (1881) triggered a chain or research which refuted this assumption. He found that one of his monkeys worked unsuccessfully for a couple of hours trying to unlock an empty trunk even though its physiological needs had been met. Marlow and Meyers (1950) found that monkeys would repeatedly unlock metal door fasteners even though they were not rewarded when successful. In working with his children, Piaget (1952) found that four- and five-month-old infants will learn to pull a string to set a suspended rattle moving; by ten months the infant will examine objects by pounding, biting, and banging them. Piaget concluded "Brighter children usually do more exploring and manipulating than duller children."

It might be tempting to conclude that the organisms described were merely relieving their boredom, but it is possible that they felt an inner urge to test the environment. In other words,

> since the earliest times man has sought to understand the world in which he lived. From the child trying to find out what makes the watch tick to the cosmologist trying to find out what makes the universe tick, man is constantly asking 'what is it?' and 'how does it work?' and 'why?' No practical benefits are required to justify this curiosity; to gain the knowledge is benefit in itself (Hill, pp. 21-22).

What motivates the organism? Simply a desire To Know.

The exploratory drive is intertwined with the curiosity drive. Berlyne (1958) studied this drive and divided it into three types. The first he called the "orienting response" which consists of adjustments the organism makes when faced with a novel situation. Such a situation might be a change in bodily stance or facial expression. Colorful and contrasting stimuli were found to elicit the most attention from infants, but it was also found that the novelty wears off quickly and stimuli must be changed frequently.

Berlyne labeled his second type of curiosity drive "locomotor exploration," which is the tendency to move about an unfamiliar environment or to manipulate a new object. He found that children tend to explore unfamiliar objects with more attention and concentration than they do familiar ones. This finding is supported by Smock and Holt (1962) who found "novelty generally evokes positive approach behavior (p. 640)." Further, they found that motivational properties vary among individuals, suggesting the presence of ontogenetic factors*.

Berlyne's third category, the "investigative," is the performance of specific activities during exploration. Berlyne conducted an interesting and informative experiment which serves as an illustration of his ideas. He placed a group of children in a darkened room, giving them access only to a key which when pressed would flash pictures on a screen. They could view the same picture as many times as they wished. He found that children soon tired of simple pattern type pictures, but they would press the key repeatedly to see complex, incongruous or startling pictures. Berlyne concluded that their only reward in this experiment was the internal satisfaction they derived from viewing the pictures.

A number of other "curiosity" experiments have been done within the last twenty-five years. A rat, for instance, free to make successive choices from the arms to a T-maze, displays a marked tendency to choose different arms on different trials. Dember (1957) found that when given a choice, rats perfer a pathway with the greatest stimulus complexity rather than the one to which they have become accustomed. In another series of experiments rats learned to solve a discrimination problem when the reward was simply the opportunity to run for a minute in a situation new to them (Montgomery and Segall, 1955). These researchers concluded that the rats were demonstrating a combined need for exploration and activity. And to satisfy those who raise the fair question "So what do rats have to do with people anyway?", Terrell found in his work with children that their need to manipulate new things in the in the environment was not related to a reward of candy.

*Factors in the course of development of an individual organism.

Glickman (1971) extended the theory that the curiosity drive is innate to show that it is so compelling it is often the undoing of an organism. For example, Darwin found that even though monkeys have a natural dread of snakes, their curiosity is so strong they will move in and look at one at close range. What is the explanation for this behavior? Glickman suggests it is a dilemma.

> ...the monkeys were caught between curiosity and fear...What can an animal gain by investigating the novel aspects of his environment and what penalties might he pay for such an investigation? A curious animal, in the right habitat, may locate new sources of food, potential mates, or choice retreats that are safe from predators. On the other hand, curiosity can distract the animal from the demands of survival and can even be physically dangerous...(Glickman, p. 55).

Interestingly enough, Glickman also found that species with less curiosity tended to show limited development of the outer mantle of brain cells that is assumed to be the source of superior intellectual ability in mammals. However, he also found that having this well-developed neocortex does not in turn assure great curiosity. Glickman's conculsion is included here as it is an appropriate statement summarizing research related to curiosity.

> We have seen some of the conditions necessary for the evolution of a curious-prone species. Ideally, such a species would demonstrate a high level of interest in novel objects along with a large repertoire of creative responses to them. A varied diet, fine manipulatory dexterity, an elegant brain with a highly developed neocortex, and relative security from predators also would contribute to the development of a most curious creature...Obviously, these factors describe our own species, *Homo sapiens* (Glickman, p. 86).

USING THE PHENOMENON OF CURIOSITY TO UNDERSTAND PROCESS

With regard to the phenomenon of curiosity, the discussion thus far has concentrated on content, that is, *what* kinds of behavior can we anticipate as a result of curiosity? If we acknowledge the plausibility of this content, the next issue becomes one of *process*. Staying with the present illustration, the question becomes: *How* can we behave so as to make it possible for the *what* or *content* of curiosity to function naturally and in ways that maximize personal growth? *How* can we increase opportunities for children's natural and innate curiosity and manipulatory and exploratory drives to flourish? In short, how can we move away from content into process?

A useful and relevant starting point is a comparison of open and closed systems. I view a closed system as one in which adults attempt to move children intellectually from Point A to Point B. This is a linear, convergent process. For example, the adult raises the question he/she wants the child to answer: "What were the causes of the American Revolution?" To supplement this process the adult supplies the child with books and other resources, answers questions, and helps the child sift through materials.

Here is the key to understanding the closed approach: Even before beginning a cognitive journey with the child, the adult knows how he/she wants it to culminate. The child will be helped to wend his/her way toward preconceived answers. Resources in the learning environment are manipulated to achieve this end. Goals and objectives are clearly defined in terms of both means and ends; the process is usually initiated and controlled by someone other than the learner.

I need not belabor a discussion of the closed approach as all are familiar with it. Most of us have been educated this way; many continue to utilize its tenets as parents and teachers. Dissatisfaction abounds with the outcomes of this process, but many educators struggle on with it assuming that the reasons for its failure lie with them. Sometimes the frustration of failure becomes unbearable and the blame is shifted to the child. "There must be something wrong with So-and-So if he/she can't get this material."

Before one can actually participate in an active process of inquiring, one must first seek information. Curiosity, the prime mover, which is most likely innate in origin, has overwhelming implications for education and personal relationships. The correlation between curiosity and process, when viewed in an open approach, demands that the roles of student and teacher and adult and child be re-evaluated.

In the closed system there exists a very definite demarcation between the teacher and student, the adult and child; it is usually the teacher-adult who contrives and/or artificially creates situations requiring an inquiry process. As previously discussed, this is unnecessary; the curiosity drive, composed of the manipulatory and exploratory drives, is already present. Much of school curriculum is geared to creating or producing curiosity when in fact it should be aimed at encouraging it. It is as if educators and parents have been busily searching for the seed to plant, often not realizing that the seed is firmly planted at birth and ready for germinating. We need not be trained biologists to know what happens to a seed deprived of sustenance.

Sadly, because most educational practices and adult-child relationships are rooted in a closed system, "the person who theorizes becomes suspect. He is viewed not only as a dreamer, but often as a *threat to the system* (Pritzkau, p. 33)." Children are not encouraged to question the what and what should be. Insight and true inquiry are usually never allowed free reign to the extent that

> in the closed system the route of inquiry is so clearly ordered that it is difficult for the individual to fail to see a mistake he has made. An implied priority in the system is that it is 'mistake proof' (Pritzkau, p. 53).

If we accept Pritzkau's contention that "curiosity is a response to uncertainty and ambiguity (p. 60)," then teachers should be trying to create a level of tension in learning situations rather than attempting to bring very different children down very similar learning paths where all the street signs are the same and where no one is encouraged to deviate from the route. If "thinking is valued above everything else (Pritzkau, p. 67)," then it is ludicrous to continue producing and buying books, games, and toys which program/dictate children's thoughts—and then congratulate ourselves, believing we are teaching children how to think!

> It appears that, in the case of children with high curiosity, it would be advantageous to present materials less rigorously balanced, less in line with their present status. In other words, high curiosity children may be more willing to accept concepts that are disturbing (Maw and Maw, p. 921).

Further, the writers suggest that certain materials are not appropriate for all children because of these differential levels of curiosity. One suggestion might be that we print books which intentionally leave every few pages or so blank. At least we might afford our students the opportunity to express what they think they are supposed to be thinking at a given time!

Educators make an interesting delineation between work and play within the confines of the classroom. "Finish all your work and you can go out for recess, use your crayons, or read a pleasure book." (A *pleasure* book, yet!) We place great emphasis on work and treat play as something which might be done after the work is completed. Basic to Piaget's application of his learning theory is recognizing the importance of play as the child uses his/her curiosity to structure reality and the environment. If "work could be defined as an extended occupation with one's curiosity, which, in reality, is play (Pritzkau, p. 72)," then perhaps educators would cease treating the satisfaction of curiosity as something that should be dealt with only after work is done.

Teachers often say, "That's an interesting thought, Joan. Why don't you look into it when you have some free time and report back to us." It is evident there are times when educators must abandon lesson plans and let everybody interested spend some time on Joan's interesting thought. Why is it that "What if...?" kinds of questions seem to be found almost exclusively in poetic domains?

It must be pointed out that the kind of expression of curiosity advocated here does not mean children flitting from one activity to another "inquiring." Children need guidance in channeling their thoughts to pick up new concepts which in turn can be extended for further growth. It is by moving into, around, and through the inquiry process that a person finds his/her intellectual identity; from this identity one is able to define his/her personal affective dimension. It is in this way and

> ...in this sense that the design of the pursuit of inquiry by the individual and his associates would enable him to approach more closely the internal 'answers' to Who am I? What am I? Why am I here? Where am I going? What is within my reach? How do I take hold of it? What remains unseen? (Pritzkau, p. 120).

A teacher was heard to comment to another teacher, immediately after the assassination of President Kennedy, that she just couldn't accomplish a thing with her class that day; all her children wanted to do was talk about the President's death and what was going on (Sarason, p. 93). Educators and all adults who interact with children need to place more importance on the phenomenon of curiosity. If they were, perhaps reactions like this teacher's would become less frequent.

We want our children to know, but we seem to want them to know only what we think they should know. Couldn't we learn to trust our children and ourselves so that we could help them learn to recognize what is worth knowing? "Curiosity killed the cat" is a big myth. It really died from lack of opportunity to be curious.

> No one asks how to motivate a baby. A baby naturally explores everything it can get at, unless restraining forces have already been at work. And this tendency doesn't die out, it's *wiped* out (Skinner, p. 123).

Process entails a systematic series of actions directed toward some desired end. Designing and implementing this systematic series of actions requires process skills which are those which have an element of ongoingness about them...In other words, although process skills are ordinarily called into play spontaneously, the individual should have the tools at his command to go back and analyze what may have transpired through more or less intuitive judgment (Berman, pp. 10-11).

An individual who uses process skills learns how to ask and answer such questions as: How did this phenomenon or behavior happen? How did this experience come to be? The ability to analyze one's behavior and experiences in this way gives the individual an enormous amount of control over his/her own life. Utilizing process skills allows one to know the ingredients of personal experiences and to better understand the experiences of others. Knowing the ingredients makes it possible to repeat positive and fulfilling experiences and to avoid negative and destructive ones.

Further, process skills have an element of ongoingness about them; they are dynamic. They are spontaneously called into action, but an individual can, in retrospect, answer such questions as: Why did I do what I did? Why did I want to do it? How did I do it? How can I do it better in the future?

The process-oriented person tries to live in an open system. He/she is willing to give others the opportunity to be the first behaver to initiate thoughts, actions, and activities. Change is a process and process will inevitably lead to change. However, many people are able to look at their interactions with others and realize that they must indeed enter into a different process if their interactions are to be enriching and worthwhile; they intuitively know that they can't have it both ways. We cannot *tell* children how to behave and at the same time expect children to learn how to behave independently and responsibly.

Many appreciate the gains to be had from learning and developing process-oriented skills, but they are at a frustrating standstill. "How do I learn these skills?" The remaining chapters deal with this crucial question.

7
And Then What?

IN THE PRECEDING chapter the subtle differences between content and process were discussed. At this point many people may be experiencing the excitement and enthusiasm for getting involved in a process of change but are feeling "I want to change *now*. I don't want to wait several weeks or months to get going on this." In this chapter I want to make two suggestions for things the now-oriented person might do while following through on some of the more time-consuming strategies discussed in Chapter 8.

STEPPING BACK

If an individual wants to be aware of the give and take in a relationship, a process I call stepping back can be easily used with immediate results. It merely requires one to be both an active participant and a passive observer in a relationship. For example, when interpersonal communication such as a verbal exchange, discussion, or interaction takes place between two people, both are active participants. In stepping back, an active participant assumes the role of passive observer and mentally relives the interaction that has transpired by asking himself/herself a series of questions: "What was actually said in our interaction?" "What was implied?" "How did I emote my feelings?" "Did I communicate my genuine feelings or was I trying to communicate an image?" "How did I camouflage my true feelings?" "Did I go out of my way to avoid any conflict, confrontation, or unpleasantness?" "Did I manipulate the other person's thoughts, ideas, and feelings?"

Stepping back and asking oneself questions such as these is not only difficult but often painful. This process tends to make us aware of the numerous roles and facades we assume in our interpersonal relationships. Stepping back also points out how very skilled we become at protecting ourselves from possible hurt and rejection. These are learned skills, unconsciously acquired through socialization; they are functional. Roles and facades help ward off potential threats to the self-esteem. They make it possible for others to get only as close to us as we deem safe, and as has been discussed throughout this book, this walling off of ourselves from others affords us a sense of control.

Stepping back makes it possible for one to be cognizant of hidden thoughts, feelings, and desires. Once they are acknowledged, they usually become trivial or at least less anxiety-provoking, and one need not invest so much time and energy in pretending they don't exist. What is particularly appealing about stepping back is that one can gain self-insight without having to share the process with anyone else. (It can even lead to a pleasant dialogue with oneself!)

All of us have developed a psychological mechanism I call a mental censor. We use this mechanism any time we mentally formulate a thought, and keep reworking it before actually verbalizing it; that is, we say it one way to ourselves, then another, and another, until we are satisfied it will elicit the result we are hoping for when it is delivered to another person. Sometimes people talk as if they were recordings; chances are their mental censors are being used. As people become skilled at giving the impression they are being spontaneous and natural, it is not so apparent that they are using their mental censors.

When we run our verbal communications through the mental censor so that we relay only thoughts and ideas which we think have a good chance of being favorably received by someone else, we are actually trying to control the relationship. If we can keep this controlled relationship on an inoffensive and innocuous level, this is all very safe. It is also very boring. The artificiality of the relationship forces us to participate in game-playing that can leave us feeling wishy-washy, insincere, guilty, and suspicious of others. If I am playing these games with another person, that I am justified in thinking he/she might in turn be playing similar games with me.

This is not to say it is desirable to rid ourselves of our mental censors. There are times when it is advantageous to have it operating at its peak level of performance. If one is making a statement to the newspaper about some sensitive issue, or if one is asked to give a testimonial about someone, the mental censor is useful. Problems result from using the mental censor in personal relationships that are of a more intimate nature—when we are communicating with those we genuinely care about—friends, family, our loved ones.

In addition to helping one understand how the mental censor inhibits full and true expression, stepping back can help one strip away the superficiality and deceit that typically get fed into relationships with those we care about. Stepping back is an initial stage in analyzing one's present communication skills.

A BEST FRIEND

For the newcomer attempting to use the stepping back process, it is imperative the right relationship be selected for scrutiny. I do not consider one's spouse necessarily a good choice as the husband-wife relationship in our society is often very intense and emotionally laden; it could be too threatening to use. On the adult-to-adult level, I think one's relationship with one's best friend is ideal to use for an initial stepping back exercise. Of all relationships, this is the one that an individual usually works the hardest at developing and nurturing.

Adults often feel locked into their relationships with their spouses and children and interactions with them often reflect a spirit of resignation and despondency. Recently I was discussing the importance of "best friend relationships" with the husband of my best friend. He felt it was implausible to try to bring some of the attributes of a relationship with a best friend to one's relationship with children. "Your ideas are ridiculous," he said. "A best friend is someone you seek out. You have things in common with a best friend."

This is exactly my point! As I suggested in an earlier chapter, it is a myth that a parent cannot be both a friend and a parent to his/her children. Discovering those processes, feelings, and behaviors which govern how we interact with a best friend can help us improve all our relationships. True, a parent cannot be a friend to children if he/she uses authority by control. However, through authority by influence, an adult can indeed bring friendship to a relationship with a child.

Two adults who are best friends rely on influencing each other; rare is the adult who would continue to be a close friend with someone who would try to control his/her behavior, morals, and values. More effort goes into trying to understand and accept the different opinions and life styles of a good friend. An adult might say to a good friend, "Hey, for whatever it's worth, I think you looked better with your hair cut short." But to a child this same adult might say, "Your hair looks dumb. Cut it or else. "

In the former statement an opinion is expressed with awareness that the recipient has feelings and the right to respond. In the latter statement the recipient of the opinion is treated off-handedly and callously. A best friend always has the option of disengaging himself/herself from a given relationship and making new friends, but the child in an adult-child relationship does not. I realize that a parent is stuck with a child just as a child is stuck with a parent, but in an adult-child relationship it is the adult who has the power to relinquish the use of control. In analyzing a relationship with a best friend it becomes apparent that individuals really work at making this relationship meaningful and worthwhile.

In my own interactions with children, I have found it useful to ask myself this question: "Would I say that to my best friend?" (Or "Would I behave that way toward my best friend?") Keeping this simple question in the back of my mind has helped me to behave with children with more sensitivity and with a willingness to view them as my equals. Also, while observing other adults interacting with children, I ask the same question. "Would he/she behave that way towards his/her best friend?" And more times than not I find myself saying, "Heh, I bet not. He/she wouldn't have that best friend for long!"

Some examples. A three-year old is watching a favorite TV show. The program will be over in ten minutes. The parent calls the child to come and eat and the child fusses because he/she wants to see the rest of the program. The parent responds with something like, "You get in here right this minute and eat. I made your dinner and I don't want any back talk from you." In a similar situation with a best friend, the same adult might respond by saying, "Well, how about bringing your dinner in front of the television, or do you want me to keep it warm until your show is over?"

Or a group of adults is engaged in conversation and a young child comes up and starts pulling on his/her mother's leg saying, "Mommy! Mommy! I have to tell you something!" A typical response I have heard is, "You interrupt once more and I will smack your bottom. Now get!" Would that same adult respond that way to a best friend? I somehow doubt it. A more typical response might be, "If what you've got on your mind can't wait, you'd better tell me!"

Another example. A child finishes using the bathtub and forgets to rinse it out, leaving the proverbial two-inch ring of dirt. The adult says to the child, "I am sick and tired of your sloppy habits. The tub always looks like Porky the Pig has wallowed in it when you get done. You're certainly old enough to clean up after yourself." Would this same adult say that to his/her best friend when the friend is a house guest? The message probably would be more along the lines of, "I really would appreciate it if you would remember to rinse out the tub when you're through."

The list of examples could go on and on. It is obvious that many adults, especially parents, treat their good friends with more dignity and consideration than they do their own children. Does this mean an adult's best friend is more important to him/her than his/her own children? Does this mean one's best friend is entitled to better treatment than one's own children?

Many parents complain that their children never talk to them. How do these same parents talk to their children? It is true that many children do not seek out their parents for conversation and advice. Likewise, it is true that many parents do not seek out their children for conversation and advice. But adults and children alike will seek out a best friend. I am not implying that children and adults can necessarily be best friends in the sense that they share common interests, activities, and ideas; rather, I am suggesting that they can share and communicate in *the ways* best friends interact with each other.

At this point many might be stifling a "Yeah but, I don't have time to treat my children the way I treat my best friend." My response is simple. Somehow we manage to find the time for a best friend.

What do we call a person attached to another by feelings of affection or personal regard? What do we call a person who gives assistance, one who is on good terms with another, one who is not hostile? The dictionary says we call such a person a friend. To be friends with children. What an exciting prospect! To make this prospect a reality means that we re-evaluate our beliefs about children's needs for authority, discipline, values and morals, and limitations. It means we need to learn effective communication skills. Being friends with children is founded on the premise, "I care about me. I care about you. I care about our relationship."

8
And What Else?

WE HAVE ALL learned How To Communicate in the strictest sense of the term. By merely living we have learned various ways to impart thoughts and ideas, transmit feelings and experiences, and make information known to others. However, few have had the opportunity to learn how to analyze the communication process. The result is that many communicate blindly without an understanding of communication skills.

In the '60s the young people of this country delivered some very loud and clear messages, a noticeable one being "Adults don't understand us." Phrases such as Communication Breakdown and Communication Gap became rallying cries. Some adults reacted with resentment, some with concern, others with indifference—but all were puzzled.

After the initial turmoil and bewilderment died down, this message from our youth was taken seriously. A concern with communication evolved. People became concerned with How am I coming across?, body language, self-fulfillment, and personal growth. "Communication Expertise" appeared in the form of books, new courses, weekend training sessions, television shows. Fads abounded and slick jargon found its way into everyday language as more and more people sought newer and better ways To Express Themselves.

Fortunately, the bandwagon effect has tapered off and we are left with a significant number of people who are interested in personal communication, not because it is the thing to do, but because they genuinely feel a need to get closer to others—to be accepted and to be more accepting of others. Words such as Openness and Honesty, which were originally adhered to with almost fanatic tenacity, are becoming more than catchy, clever vocabulary. For a variety of reasons more people are re-evaluating their lives, taking stock of more readily available personal and professional options, and concluding, "Yes, I think I can be much more than I presently am; I can do more than I previously thought possible; I can have more satisfying relationships."

Yes, many do desire to grow in new directions, in new areas. But to grow means to change. It is at this point that many dreams either remain at the fantasy level or fade completely. It is not enough to *say,* "I want to have more open and honest relationships." It can get very lonely and frightening even contemplating a move from the *say* stage to the *do* stage. Most of us need some solid and practical assistance in this process.

The recent emphasis on scrutinizing personal communication has helped facilitate a change/growth process for many. More people are realizing that all relationships are only as good as the communication skills that feed them. But what are some of the alternatives available to those who are concerned about their personal relationships, especially those with children? Specifically, how does one go about developing better communication skills?

COMMUNICATION SKILLS CAN BE RELEARNED

Communication skills are acquired beginning the first day of life, usually unconsciously through imitation and modeling. A child is exposed to his/her parents' style of communication; he/she incorporates and internalizes facets of this style into his/her own. It is therefore not surprising that adults who yell a lot at children in turn have children who yell a lot at them. Parents who are more low-key and even in disposition usually raise children who are similarly disposed. This is not a hard and fast rule, of course, as one's ways of communicating are the result of a complicated network* of phenomena, but for the most part children do pattern their own patterns of communication after adults important to them in their early years, and after peers in their later years.

As a corollary to the fact that communication skills are learned, it must be stressed that one can analyze present communication skills and learn new ones to replace inadequate or unsatisfactory ones. Both these steps are a tremendous undertaking and it is a rare person who can proceed successfully on his/her own.

I emphasize this point because frustrated sets of parents often delude themselves into thinking that because they care about each other and their children, they can solve all their interpersonal

---

*Picking up on this word, I shudder to think how extensive and pervasive the influence of television has been on acquired communication skills!

communication problems. This reasoning is unrealistic and further compounds the situation. "There must be something wrong with us. We're working so hard at talking with each other and the children, and nothing seems to be changing." Chances are that nothing significant is happening because they are confronting problems with the same skills they have always used; it is likely that these very skills were a major component creating the problems in the first place! A sincere intention for change in relationships is a prerequisite, but this is merely a necessary mindset, the first step, the motivating factor.

For example, if two people committed to a relationship decided they want to learn how to play good tennis as opposed to using their self-taught tennis, what would they do? Obviously they would want to work with someone who is skilled at tennis. However, the fact that they have located a competent tennis player is no guarantee that this person can teach others how to play. Shopping around for the right teacher is a necessity—one must find a person who possesses both the tennis skills and teaching skills. No one would dispute the fact that not everyone is qualified to teach our hypothetical couple how to play good tennis.

I would like to extend this same example to the area of communication skills. If one wants to learn the in's and out's of the process of communicating, including both *what* is communicated to others and *how* it is done, then one needs to shop around to find someone who is trained and proficient in teaching these skills. It is at this point that many get defensive and start screaming "Oh rubbish! There's nothing wrong with the way I get my ideas across. It's just that the people I have to deal with are so stubborn and dense that they don't understand me."

Without belaboring the point I would suggest that men are more apt to have this attitude than are women. Concern with nurturing relationships has traditionally been considered feminine behavior, and many males have great difficulty in admitting failure in their personal relationships. (We owe our gratitude to the many men and women who are participating in the feminist movement. They are helping make it easier for both genders to speak up when their personal relationships are causing emotional pain.) Many people, especially some men, would view themselves as weak individuals if they sought help in improving their communication skills.

THE EMOTIONAL PHANTOM

We all know people who feel that if one can't help himself/herself in all areas of existence, then that person is emotionally decrepit. It is next to impossible to get close to those who believe this because they deliberately keep us affectively distant from them. I call such people "emotional phantoms," and I use the term descriptively, not derogatorily.

Emotional phantoms drift in and out of relationships—they let people get close to them in certain ways, but they keep other parts of themselves walled off. We can discuss safe topics with them— How is your job going? How are you going to spend your vacation?—but other areas are taboo. We may want to tell them that we feel distant from them, or that we fear they resent us, or maybe just that we love them, but to broach such feelings with them often puts a strain on the relationship. They get uncomfortable, and deny that anything is amiss, or make light of what we are trying to say. They usually leave us feeling embarrassed for bringing up such thoughts in the first place.

Unfortunately, the emotional phantom usually gets his/her way. Certain areas of the relationship remain untouched with an implied message that "I just won't get into certain topics with you." (Scrutinizing these "certain topics" usually reveals that it is the area of *feelings* that is off limits.) This is not to suggest that the emotional phantom lacks skill in communicating. Quite the contrary! He/she is in fact extremely skillful at determining the course of a relationship via the communication process, keeping a distance in the relationship, and controlling another's input into the relationship. The correlation between control and instilling feelings of guilt has already been discussed; suffice it to say that it is difficult if not impossible to develop a truly satisfying relationship with someone who is locked into emotional phantomdom.

The children of emotional phantoms, like other children, model the communication skills used by important adults, especially their parents. This modeling-imitation includes many inappropriate and ineffective skills. Children learn to be emotional phantoms at a young age and in turn teach their children this same communicating style. The cycle is obvious and must be broken.

GO IT ALONE

I have often heard one spouse say of the other, "I really do want to improve my communication skills, but my husband/wife thinks I am being silly." My response to this is very simple: go it alone. It certainly would be convenient to have someone important join in the analysis-relearning process, but often the people we really care about are not motivated to do so. As is the case with the emotional phantom, they are often motivated to do all they can to make sure that others around them don't change, especially if they feel a need to be in control of their personal relationships.

It is scapegoating another to say "I would get some assistance in improving my communication skills if only so-and-so would do it with me." This is putting an unfair burden on the other person. Back to the example of the couple wanting to learn how to play tennis: it would be ridiculous for one to insist that the other take lessons if he/she weren't interested in doing so. Also, it would be destructive to the relationship to say "I won't take the lessons unless you do." The hidden message is "I know you don't want to," but if you really love me...." This kind of pressure is manipulative and intolerable.

Similarly, it would be anxiety-provoking and a source of tremendous resentment to apply that same kind of pressure on another with regard to learning new communication skills. All one can do is suggest to the other that learning new communication skills together might improve their own relationship, improve their relationships with their children, or that it might be fun and different to do something special together. But all such reasons must be delivered as a request, not a demand that is going to be the source of hassling.

Once a person is motivated to learn new communication skills and is committed to actually doing so, then the shopping around process must take place. In the remainder of this chapter I discuss some options one might consider. Some people have been gratified by using just one of the suggested courses of action, while others have found it beneficial to use two or more of the alternatives at different times. As is the case with shopping around for anything, it is easy to become discouraged and disheartened, but if the motivation and commitment are strong enough, a satisfactory approach will be found.

A final point of caution. I think many people naively hope learning new communication skills is going to take care of each and every problem they must deal with. This just isn't going to happen. Learning new skills can be an active, positive way of coping with the struggles of daily living, but some problems are inevitable and will always exist. Learning better ways of communicating will not make life problem-free; it may help in making problems more manageable and in helping people feel better about themselves and their potential. I offer the options not as panaceas, but as ways that many have found helpful and effective for enriching personal growth and relationships with others.

Formal Courses For Learning Communication Skills

Many people are fortunate enough to live within commuting distance of either universities, four-year colleges, or community colleges. Almost all of these offer relevant courses for learning about the communication process. Such courses might be titled Communication Skills, Effective Communication, Values and Communication, Values Clarification, or the like. Each college's catalogue will list courses and their descriptions. However, course catalogues are not always up-to-date. A supplementary list of course offerings is sometimes available and can be obtained by contacting the institution and requesting both the catalogue and a list of "add-on" courses. For example, one college in my own area recently undertook a massive publicity campaign to inform the public that they were offering an extensive series on Parenting led by different experts. This course was not listed in their catalogue.

I have learned from numerous participants in workshops in which I talk about college courses as an option that making that first call to a college or university can arouse much anxiety, especially for people who are not in contact with the campus scene. (I know a woman who spent eight months thinking about getting a catalogue before she actually did anything about obtaining it.) Granted, learning about course offerings can be a difficult task, but it is a necessary first step in this process. For some it will require a determined gritting of the teeth and doing it!

I have also heard this comment many times: "I only have a high school diploma, so I can't just sign up for a college course." This is not necessarily so. Many college courses are open to anyone who can pay the tuition. Some colleges do require that students be matriculating to enroll in courses, but they usually also offer Continuing Education courses. Continuing Ed. courses have been designed for those who do want to take courses but have no firm intention of working towards a degree. Community colleges are particularly sensitive to encouraging all people to enroll, regardless of their academic background or future plans.

Lest anyone think I am implying that only laypeople can profit from taking Communication Skills courses, I want to say a word or two about professionals—educators, social workers, psychologists, and the like. Some of the least effective communicators I have ever come across are people whose den walls are draped with academic degrees. College degrees, undergraduate or graduate, are no guarantee that their holders are skilled in communicating. In fact, I think many institutions of higher learning have been negligent in not requiring at least one course in communication skills as an integral part of every program, especially teacher training. (I know some administrators who could also profit from such courses!)

I have taught communication skills to three different groups of people—parents, student teachers, and teachers. It has been my experience that student teachers are the most receptive to the idea that an analysis-relearning of skills can help them become better teachers and happier people in general. Without a doubt I have found student teachers an absolute joy to work with in this area. They are fresh, truly alive, and not as fearful of change as others.

Working with parents has also been rewarding and fun for me. Although they tend to resist the process initially, once they realize that acquiring new communication skills does not mean they should feel guilty about their old ones, they also get immersed in the process with exuberance and commitment.

Teaching communication skills to teachers has been grueling and frustrating for me. I have found them to be defensive about their present skills, resistive to change, and at times almost contemptuous toward the suggestion that everyone can improve his/her ways of communicating with others. Upon questioning, several teachers have avowed that since they view themselves as professionals they feel they shouldn't need help in this area. They are wrong about this. Period.

Unfortunately, once someone is actually enrolled in a course such as Communication Skills or Values Clarification, there is not always a nice match between course outcomes and the expectations of the student. It is advantageous to talk with someone who has already taken the same course with the same instructor, but this is not always possible. The direction, focus, and course outcomes are primarily determined by the person teaching or facilitating the course, but such prior knowledge is not always forthcoming.

So, we end up in courses where we are delighted, reasonably satisfied, or discouraged—and sometimes damned angry when we think about the tuition we've sunk into them! There simply are no guarantees in this business.

Once a course is underway, many instructors are receptive to and even encourage input from class members. If a person taking a course is feeling somewhat disappointed in either the content of the course of the way it is being taught, he/she can discuss this disappointment with the instructor and/or other people enrolled. When this discussion is handled with sensitivity and consideration, most instructors will try to gear the course to meeting individual needs that are possible and appropriate.

Sometimes a particular course someone wants to take is not offered. In this case it is a good idea to itemize exactly what one is looking for. A list such as the following might be developed. "I am looking for a course which will help me:

1. learn how to analyze my ways of communicating;
2. learn how to listen and be more responsive to others;
3. learn how my verbal behavior affects others;
4. understand why children communicate in the ways in which they do;
5. learn more about the stages of child growth and development;
6. appreciate how responses affect different situations."

Of course, such a list will be different for each individual, depending upon what he/she is looking for.

It might also be beneficial for two or more friends who have decided to take a course together to generate a collective list. This composite outline of needs can then be used in a couple of ways. It might be used in trying to locate a course already being offered. Sitting down with the Registrar, a faculty member, or an administrator, and going over it together will help them determine which existing course will best meet their needs; or if such a course is not presently offered, such a list can assist college personnel in creating new courses.

The cost for taking a course will vary from tree to very expensive, depending upon the institution. Paying more for a course is not an indicator that the course will be better than one which costs less.

Taking a college or university course, then, has proven a successful option for many people interested in improving their communication skills. Many have found meeting the other people in the course has been as fruitful and rewarding as the course itself. If one's daily contacts are primarily with people who are not particularly concerned with the self-growth and personal fulfillment that can result from learning more about communication processes, it is easy to abandon this goal. However, by getting involved in a college or continuing education course which focuses on communication, one will be in immediate contact with others who share similar interests.

PARENT TRAINING PROGRAMS

Another approach which many adults have found useful in improving communication skills and enhancing relationships, especially those involving children, is parent training programs. I will mention three such programs that are available in given locales and then I will give a more detailed description of another which is available nationally.

In the Los Angeles area there is a program called Parent Involvement Program (P.I.P.). (Acronyms are such fun!) This parent training program has been developed by experts to be used by ordinary parents with ordinary children. Anyone who has interacted with children knows there is no such thing as an "ordinary child!" The term is used to differentiate this kind of a program from those which are developed specifically for parents who have children with special needs, such as coping problems or handicaps.

Although the programs discussed here may have the potential to be effective with children with special needs, they are mentioned as examples of programs which are geared to helping parents interact with children who have the usual problems resulting from child growth and development.

In Kansas City the Responsive Parent Training Program is available. This program teaches parents the use of standard modification techniques including an understanding of the theory of behavior modification and devising and implementing these techniques in everyday situations.

In Chicago at the Alfred Adler Institute, Children: The Challenge study groups are available. Psychologist Rudolf Dreikurs has taken many of the ideas of Alfred Adler (1870-1937, founder of Individual Psychology) and translated them for practical use by parents.

Adults living in Los Angeles, Kansas City, and Chicago have the option of investigating the three above-mentioned parent training programs. Others have the option of looking into the most nationally well-known parent training program, Parent Effectiveness Training (P.E.T.). As a certified instructor of this program, I feel qualified to give a more detailed description of this approach, including its advantages and disadvantages.

PARENT EFFECTIVENESS TRAINING

Dr. Thomas Gordon, a clinical psychologist, is the founder of Effectiveness Training.* In his therapy with children of all ages, Gordon found they were all voicing a similar complaint: "My parents don't understand me," "My folks won't listen to me," "I can't talk with my mother and father." Gordon focused on this apparent communication problem; he discovered that the children were indeed correct, to a certain extent. Many parents simply did not know how to talk with their children in productive and meaningful ways. Many of these parents had never learned some basic communication skills which would enhance and expand the exchange of thoughts, feelings, and ideas.

In an attempt to help all adults learn better communication skills, Parent Effectiveness Training was developed, marketed, and is now nationally available. At this writing about 250,000 adults have completed the course. It is a proprietary enterprise— the product being sold is communication skills. It is fundamentally a good product, but I point out a major caution.

At present there are approximately 8,000 certified P.E.T. instructors. Unfortunately, a screening process for certification of these instructors is virtually non-existent; almost anyone with a college degree can pay his/her money to attend a training workshop. This training last for five days, after which the newly certified instructor can return to his/her community and begin teaching the course.

Obviously the quality of the instructors ranges from superb to poor and this variation can be found within a given community. It is imperative that anyone considering taking this course obtain prior knowledge of the competency of the person teaching it. Word-of-mouth is the quickest and most accurate way to get this information. One should ask the instructor for a list of the members in his/her last class and call a random few for an up-front appraisal of the course and instructor.

---

*In addition to Parent Effectiveness Training, Teacher Effectiveness Training (T.E.T.) and Leadership Effectiveness Training (L.E.T.) are also offered. The skills taught in all three courses are basically the same.

During the course, members attend class one night a week for eight weeks. Each class meets for three hours—a total of twenty-four hours. The content of the course includes lectures, discussions, tapes, and realistic practice of the skills. The tuition ranges from $50 to $70, depending upon geographic location. The instructor receives a set portion of this tuition; the remainder goes to Effectiveness Training Associates.

Although the particular course under discussion here is called Parent Effectiveness Training, it could just as accurately be called People Effectiveness Training. The skills taught are not limited to adult-child interactions; most class members find they are able to use the skills in all their communications.

An overview of the skills taught in this course can help familiarize readers with what is meant by learning new communication skills. Although the skills taught will vary from one communication skills course to another, a consideration of the P.E.T. skills can help one gain an appreciation of what is meant by a "communication-process skills approach."

Parent Effectiveness Training Skills

In P.E.T. the group first considers the concept of problem ownership. For example, if a child comes steaming into the house and announces that he/she hates school and is going to run away, an adult's typical and immediate thought is, "Oh, oh. *We* have a problem." The concerned adult usually responds with such statements as: "Oh, have a fresh brownie. It'll make you feel better," "School isn't all that bad." "You need an education so you can get a good job. " "Why don't you call So-and-So to come over to take your mind off things."

What often happens is that the adult, who is genuinely concerned about the child, jumps in with both feet and takes on the child's problem as if it were his/her own and works madly to make everything all right again. The basic questions are: Who owns this problem? Who is directly bothered by it? To help answer these questions, twelve roadblocks to communication are defined. These common readblocks include: ordering; warning; preaching; giving solutions; lecturing; judging; praising; name-calling; interpreting; consoling; questioning; and humoring.

We all use them at one time or another with the intent of helping another solve a problem. But upon careful scrutiny, it becomes apparent that these roadblocks inhibit communication; they inadvertently and subtly tell a child that he/she seems incapable of solving his/her own problems. The person who originally voiced the problem suddenly becomes the listener when the roadblocks are used. "Now just hold still and let me tell you what you should be feeling and doing about this situation" is the message that is relayed.

The next logical question then becomes: "Okay, if I accept that the roadblocks to communication work against my relationships with others, what can I do? The roadblocks are all I know." The answer to this question is active-listening, a set of learned skills in which the concerned listener feeds back to the person with the problem the *feelings* he/she thinks the person with the problem is emoting. "Gee, it sounds like you had a positively rotten day at school." The child with the problem might respond with, "Oh boy, did I ever!" or "No. School was okay. It was on the way home that such-and-such happened...."

Active-listening makes it possible for the child with the problem to discuss his/her feelings about it without interference from an adult. After the feelings have been aired, children can demonstrate their ability to solve their problems themselves. The active-listening skills are interpreted by a child to mean that the adult is saying: "I really care that you are bothered and upset by your problem. I want to help and I can best do that by feeding back to you what I hear you saying and emoting. I have enough trust in you to know that you are capable of coming up with solutions which will best satisfy your needs."

The active-listening skills require practice, practice, and more practice. Because of our own socialization and backgrounds, it is very natural to slip in those roadblocks; it takes practice not to use them. Without an in-depth appreciation of the roadblocks and active-listening skills, many adults assume that this approach reflects parental-adult irresponsibility. Much thought is given to this concept of parental responsibility and problem ownership; many times adults find that they have incorporated into their realm of responsibility goals which are inhumanly possible.

Many adults worry about consistency. An internal voice frequently blasts at them: "You should be consistent in your interactions with children." This is a fallacy. Situations change, needs change, people's feelings change, even from one moment to the next. The human organism is in a constant state of flux. Consequently, it is unrealistic to strive for consistency of behavior. It is realistic, however, to strive for openness and honesty in communication. An adult can learn how to be as non-threatening as possible when communicating feelings to a child.

For example, many confuse being consistent with enforcing rigid and tiresome rules. "You may not play the stereo after eight o'clock at night." Such a decree can become a problem in terms of actual enforcement; a child who is told this over and over again can build up resentment towards the adult. This accrued resentment will surface in other facets of the relationship. This approach to consistency never gets at the feelings behind the rule. It is much more realistic and relationship-oriented to say, "Last night your stereo didn't bother me. I had a good day and I rather enjoyed the music. Tonight I have a headache and the music is bothering me. We have to work out a solution." The consistency is with process rather than with content—the process is one of being consistently honest and open with others.

In active-listening the other person owns the problem. However, there are numerous occasions when someone's behavior causes someone else to be troubled. For example, a child who keeps a messy room and just revels in wallowing in dirty laundry, strewn books, and open dresser drawers does not own a problem. The parent who looks at the room and sees red owns a problem. What to do?

I -Messages are the skills used to relay to the other person, "Hey, what you are doing is causing me great consternation. I want you to know how it makes me feel and why." The responsibility for change is left with the other person causing the problem. I-Messages suggest that both parties have needs which must be defined. Both parties learn how individual behavior often has an effect on others.

I say to our daughter Heather, "I really resent it when you call me in the middle of the night to hand you your water cup because this interferes with my sleep." This I-Message lets Heather know how her behavior is affecting me and that it does in fact cause a problem for me. It also lets her know that it is up to her to assume the responsibility for changing her behavior. She is learning to reach over and grab her water cup and I try to acknowledge this with a positive I-Message of appreciation in the morning. "I really appreciate it when you get your own water without calling me because then I can get a good night's sleep." Sometimes she forgets and still calls me, but I feel we are making headway with this problem.

At any rate, I am much more comfortable sending an I-Message than bellowing at her in the middle of the night, "Reach over and get your own cup and quit being such a nuisance." I lost my patience one night and I did holler at her. She cried for ten minutes until I went in and apologized to her for treating her in such an insensitive and callous way. Appropriate skills make it possible to communicate an apology, feelings of anger or impatience, or a need to be separated from another; the key is in communicating in ways that carry the least risk of devastating the other person while at the same time getting one's own needs met. These same skills also make it possible to share feelings of love, joy, and delight without feeling embarrassed or awkward about doing so.

Many people first exposed to communication skills say,"All that reasoning with children is ridiculous." I have a stereotypic image that comes to mind when I hear this. I picture a frightened looking adult pleading with a kid saying, "Now, sweet precious, let's be reasonable about this. I know you are angry, but it hurts me when you kick me in the shins." Further, my stereotype suggests that the adult "trying to be reasonable" is terrified of the child and really is at a loss about how to interact. I suspect that there are others who share this image with me of what is meant by being reasonable with children.

Let me stress right here and now that using communication skills does not mean becoming subservient to children. It does not mean the adult uses a sweet tone of voice when he/she really is annoyed with a child. It does not mean the adult disguises negative feelings towards the child or pretends that the child is all sweetness and goodness when in fact, at that moment, the adult really feels that the child is the most obnoxious human being ever to stalk the earth. Using appropriate communication skills does mean that interactions transpire without pleading and cajoling. Genuine feelings are communicated accurately.

Another question often asked with regard to communication skills is: "Aren't these skills geared to interactions with older children, children who have a good grasp of language?" Most definitely not. Such skills can be used very effectively even with toddlers and infants. Granted, a toddler's repertoire of responses is more limited, but from the moment of birth an adult can interact with a baby using the skills, confident that a foundation of communication based on mutual trust and concern is being built.

Toddlers can begin to realize that all people have needs. "Heather, I can see that you want to go outside right now, but I have to make a phone call first." A young child is more apt to react positively to this response, especially if this kind of process is used consistently, than to a reply of "No. We aren't going outside now.

Go play with your train." We have all witnessed a toddler's response to this. Whimpering, (the books say to ignore it), then crying, (the books say to ignore it), and finally, in some cases, a full-fledged tantrum, (the books are not in agreement as to the right reaction to this).

However, using process skills can help alleviate such potentially upsetting situations because the emphasis is on knowing *how* to express feelings and what to do with these feelings once they have been expressed. Children of all ages appreciate openness and honesty in communication. An additional benefit is that over a period of time they in turn learn to be open and honest and considerate of other people's needs and rights.

This makes it possible for eight-year-old Ben to say to his mother in the midst of a squabble with his younger brother, "Mom, I really don't see that this is your problem." In this particular case Mom agreed and left while the two brothers worked through their difficulty (successfully). If the boys' behavior was causing this mother a problem, if she was disturbed by their bickering, she would have been able to use an I-Message to inform them of this. It is apparent that the children in this family are learning how to use process-communication skills through their interactions with a mother who employs them. The process is self-perpetuating.

In all relationships many situations arise in which neither party owns the problem; that is, the relationship owns the problem. For example, it is Saturday morning and Father wants to spend the morning doing the weekly grocery shopping. Child wants to spend the morning at the zoo with Father. This is called a conflict-of-needs situation.

A set of skills for this conflict-of-needs situation is taught which is unlike the compromise approaches sometimes used. In a compromise, at least one party, if not all parties, sacrifices some or all of his/her needs. Once in a great while an agreeable compromise can be reached, especially if an entire family is involved, but for the most part, compromises usually result in someone's feeling short-changed. "We always end up doing what So-and-So wants to do. We never do what I want to do."

The suggested conflict-of-needs skills are designed so that everyone feels satisfied after working through the process. In some situations the process must be worked through more than once because someone does not hold up his/her end of the agreement which has been reached. The underlying tenets of the skills imply that no one need feel dissatisfied with an agreement or feel that he/she is losing more than is being gained. An atmosphere is created in which adult and child alike learn to recognize an actual or potential conflict-of-needs situation; both also learn to instigate the use of the skills by saying, "We have (or are going to have) a problem and we need to talk about it." A solution agreeable to all involved is the goal, e.g., Father and Child grocery shop in the morning and go to the zoo in the afternoon.

The steps in resolving a conflict-of-needs include defining needs; generating, evaluating, and implementing solutions; and re-evaluating the process whenever necessary. It is initially time-consuming to go through these steps, but when they are practiced and used regularly, people do learn how to facilitate the steps and focus on only the relevant issues. Involved parties also learn to trust each other through the use of the process skills so that no one need fear being ripped off in a conflict-of-needs situation.

Many issues can't be analyzed as he/she owns the problem (use active-listening); I own the problem (send an I-Message); or our relationship owns the problem (conflict-of-needs skills needed). Issues which do not fall into any of these categories might be a child's style of dress, choice of friends, or use of leisure time. These kinds of issues fall into the area of values. Values must be defined, both generally and as they are specifically related to individuals. Consideration must be given to the relationship between a person's own values and the acceptance of another person's values. Values clarification can help one make his/her values meaningful and important to another, but it is vital to realize that the modification of values is ultimately a matter of individual choice.

In short, the skills taught in Parent Effectiveness Training have the potential to help personal communication become an integrated, productive, and purposeful aspect of relationships, especially the adult-child relationship. Again I emphasize that the capabilities of the instructors vary enormously and it is imperative that anyone thinking about taking this course* get some feedback about the instructor and his/her teaching of the skills from people who have actually taken the course. Learning these skills from a qualified and competent person can be an exciting and effective way of improving one's communication.

*To learn more about the course and to receive the name(s) of certified instructors in a given community, contact Effectiveness Training Associates. Address is included in the Bibliography.

USING ESTABLISHED MEMBERSHIP TO LEARN COMMUNICATION SKILLS

Utilizing other community resources to learn communication-process skills requires more initiative and imagination than taking a college course or a parent-training program. Signing up for a course requires making a phone call or two, registering, making payment, and attending the scheduled class meetings. Tapping other community resources often requires making numerous phone calls, attending some worthwhile and some not-so worthwhile meetings, and working with people whose interest will range from "very" to "sometimes" to "not at all." And with this less than exuberant introduction, I want to present some options to be considered.

Many people are already active members in organized groups such as a PTA or PTO (Parent-Teacher Association or Parent-Teacher Organization), New-Comers (for people new to a town or community), religious organizations, single-parent groups, community-action groups, and the like. At one time or another most organizations or community groups bring in outside people either to give a lecture, a workshop, or conduct a seminar. A group member could suggest bringing in a trained person to teach communication skills to the entire membership or just to those interested.

One way to locate someone qualified to teach these skills is to contact a college or university for a list of possibilities, or get in touch with talented public school educators who have demonstrated expertise in this area. Some organizations have a treasury and are able to offer remuneration for such services; others must depend upon the generosity of volunteers. I have some very strong feelings about using volunteers which I would like to interject.

I believe that educators are often taken advantage of when it comes to giving workshops and other presentations that are not part of their regular employment. My experience has suggested that many people feel educators somehow "owe them" the benefit of their expertise; educators should feel it is a privilege to be asked to work with various groups. Part of this feeling probably stems from an attitude of "Well, for what we are paying in taxes for education, we should get more than we already are."* I can sympathize with the aggravation resulting from increasing

---

*With today's excess of qualified teachers, I also suspect that many people have the attitude a teacher should be grateful to have a position and he/she should show this gratitude by volunteering time and talents to the community.

taxes—I pay them also. However, if a group were inviting in an attorney or a brain surgeon to teach a course requiring several meetings, I daresay that the group would not expect this lawyer or doctor to do it out of the goodness of his/her heart. The group would expect to pay, in most cases, a significant sum for this instruction.

I think this attitude should be extended more than it is to include educators. Granted, in many cases our taxes do provide their salaries, and to a certain extent it is correct to view them as "public servants" of sorts, but this term does not mean "subservient" to the public's every need. We do not own educators and they do not owe us anything beyond their very best contribution during their hours of employment. Whenever possible, they deserve to be paid for their time and talents utilized outside of regular employment.

If payment for outside speakers is a problem, then the creative energies of the group should be geared towards ways of making it worthwhile for the outsider to come in and instruct. In those situations where payment is to be minimal (or impossible!), I suggest the following to entice qualified people to teach communication skills to groups.

Getting Qualified Speakers While Keeping Costs Down
One way is to contact graduate departments of colleges and universities and inquire if there are any Masters or Doctoral candidates doing thesis or dissertation research in humanistic or educational psychology; one of them might be willing to teach communication skills in return for help from the group members in collecting data or being the population used in a study.

Another possibility is to contact public school systems, colleges, or universities and ask to speak to the people responsible for writing their state and/or federal proposals for grants. Often the regulations for receiving grants require community involvement and it might be possible to establish a symbiotic relationship between the institution and the group. The group could offer to be a source of community involvement in a funded project in return for some qualified person to teach communication skills to the group.

It might be possible for a PTA or a PTO to apply directly for funding for a model program in which parents and teachers work together towards the implementation of a common goal. (Some of the sources which might be interested in such a proposal are the National Institute of Education, National Institute of Child

Health and Human Development, Office of Child Development, Office of Education, and Department of Health, Education, and Welfare.) One of the proposal objectives or activities could be learning communication skills; the proposal budget could include a request for money to pay someone to teach these skills. If the option of funding is considered, it is obvious that the group would have to consult someone familiar with the Federal Register to know what monies are available and how to apply for them.

Another possibility utilizing the combined efforts of parents and teachers is that of sending a teacher or administrator to an appropriate place such as a college course or a communications skills workshop for training at the expense of the PTA, PTO, or school system. This person could in turn teach communication skills to parent-teacher groups and in-service teacher groups. If parents vocalize their need for this kind of help and also their desire to work with their children's teachers in learning skills to improve relationships, it is possible that monies could be found in tightening school budgets to meet this need.

Obviously, just a few people voicing this need probably would not make administrators or a school committee sit up and take notice; however, a petition with many signatures or a vociferous vote at a meeting in favor of a communication skills course could convince many of the right people that there is a genuine need in this area. The key to making this approach work is convincing as many as possible that it is to everyone's advantage—children, parents, teachers, administrators, all members of the community—to work collectively and cooperatively in improving modes of communication.

The last possibility I would like to suggest is that of contacting retired educators in the community to see if one of them already has or would be interested in acquiring communication skills training (preferably at the group's expense!), and teach these skills to the group. Many retired teachers and administrators would appreciate having an opportunity to use their talents and expertise in this way.

Taking advantage of one's membership in an established organization or community group, then, is one way of realizing the goal of learning better ways of communicating. Once the desire or need is stated, "This group wants to learn about communication processes and skills," the group can brainstorm different possibilities taking into account such factors as monies available, willingness of people to contribute time and money, and the various resources to be tapped. Besides the obvious benefits of acquiring useful skills, there is the additional benefit of the group participating in a process which can generate tremendous *esprit de corps* . The group members can become a closer and more cooperatively functioning unit as they grow together in new ways.

OPTIONS AVAILABLE ON AN INDIVIDUAL BASIS

In addition to utilizing one's membership in a group or organization to learn communication skills, there are some alternatives open to the individual who is not a member of a group. The most obvious and perhaps most expedient course of action is to join a group and use the suggestions discussed in the previous section. The benefits of "comfort in numbers" are apparent. However, many people prefer to strike out *a cappella* on an adventure such as learning new communication skills— without the accompaniment of people they know. This heartier type might find success in doing one or more of the following.

First, one might run an ad in the personal sections of newspapers asking people interested in forming a group to learn communication skills to contact him/her. (I have never tried this approach, so I can't vouch for who might turn up as "interested people," but I'm sure it would be fascinating!) If enough people respond, they can form a group and brainstorm ways to attain their goals.

Second, one can follow newspapers and community bulletin boards (supermarkets, libraries) for notices of open meetings that are focusing on topics such as parental roles, interacting with children, and communication skills. Attending this kind of meeting can at least put one in the same room with others who might share similar interests. My own town recently sponsored an all-day Saturday workshop featuring a well-known psychologist/writer as the keynote speaker. Small-group workshops were conducted throughout the day pertaining to family life and improving relationships. Perhaps a few appropriately placed phone calls or letters to newspaper editors, town officials, or educators could result in more communities sponsoring similar events. The one in my town was a huge success and is serving as a model for other towns.

Third, one can get involved in group or individual therapy. I am quick to add that for a couple of reasons I am somewhat reluctant to suggest this option. Therapy can be very expensive.

Also, many people have inaccurate ideas about who can profit from therapy and what actually goes on during it. I do not want to get side-tracked by a lengthy discussion of the different kinds of therapy or the merits or disadvantages of each type, but I do want to say that the right therapeutic situation with the right therapist can allow one a unique opportunity to learn about one's true feelings, goals and aspirations, in effective ways of coping with stress, and better interaction skills. Finding this therapist and matching him/her with financial considerations requires a shopping expedition of its own.

Possible ways to find a good therapist include talking with friends who have had positive experiences with one, calling community health centers, following leads in newspapers or magazines, and calling certified psychologists/psychiatrists listed in the yellow pages of the phone book. Inevitably the therapist will say, "And why do you think you might want to get involved in therapy?" One can reply, "Because I am not satisfied with the ways in which I communicate with others and I want to improve these skills." A good therapist can help one acquire these skills or make suggestions for other ways to acquire them.

From the various suggestions made throughout this chapter it is obvious that the process I am advocating—learning better communication skills—requires time, patience, stamina, and in some cases, money. There are no rosy paths to take, there are no quick answers, and there are no "ten easy steps to follow." We have all experienced the frustration of inadequate communication; hopefully more people will commit themselves to bettering their interaction-communication skills. It is often a long and painful process, but it can also be the most worthwhile and enriching experience of one's life.

AND . . .

As caring educators and parents our task is twofold: we must re-evaluate *what* we want to bring to our relationships with children and *how* to interact with success and sensitivity. It is a task of tremendous magnitude, but it must be done, and must be done now. And no YEAH BUTS about it.

Bibliography

Aries, Philippe. *Centuries of Childhood: A Social History of Family Life.* Robert Baldick, trans. New York: Vintage Books, 1960.

Bereiter, Carl. "The Right to Make Mistakes." *Intellect,* 1973, December, 102: 184-190.

Berlyne, D.E. "Novelty and Curiosity as Determinants of Exploratory Behavior." *British Journal Of Psychology, 1958, 41: 68-60.*

Berman, Louise M. *New Priorities in the Curriculum.* Columbus, Ohio: Charles E. Merrill Publishing Co., 1968.

Bloom, Benjamin. *Stability and Change in Human Characteristics.* New York: Wiley, 1964.

Brothers, Joyce. "How to Avoid Being an Indulgent Parent." *Good Housekeeping,* 1973, October, 70ff.

Coopersmith, Stanley. "Studies In Self-Esteem." Scientific American, 1968, February, 218:96-105.

Cox, James. "Help Your Child to Self-Esteem." *Today's Health,* 1968, February, 24ff.

Dember, D.N. "Response by Rats to Differential Stimulus Complexity," *Journal of Physiological Psychology,* 1957, 50:514-518.

Effectiveness Training Associates, 531 Stevens Avenue, Solana Beach, California 91101. (714-481-8121)

Eliasberg, Ann P. "How to Make the Most of Your Parent Power." *Parents' Magazine*, 1974, March, 40ff.

Erikson, Erik H. *Childhood and Society*. New York: Norton & Company, 1963.

Farson, Richard. *Birthrights*. New York: Macmillan, 1974a.

Farson, Richard. "Are You Oppressing Your Children?" *Forbes*, 1974b, January, 113, 34-38.

Farson, Richard. "Birthrights," *Ms. Magazine*, 1974c, March, 66ff.

Ferm, Deane Williams. "The New Morality." *Parents' Magazine*, 1968, May, 38.

Glanzer, Murray. "Curiosity, Exploratory Drive, And Stimulous Satiation." *Psychology Bulletin*, 1958, 55:302-315.

Glickman, Stephen E. "Curiosity Has Killed More Mice Than Cats." *Psychology Today*, 1971, October, 54ff.

Goldenson, Robert M. *The Encyclopedia of Human Behavior: Psychology, Psychiatry, and Mental Health*. New York: Doubleday & Co., 1970.

Gordon, Thomas. *Parent Effectiveness Training: The Tested New Way to Raise Responsible Children*. New York: Weyden, 1970.

Graves, C.W. "The Deterioration of Work Standards." *Harvard Business Review*, 1966, 44:120ff.

Grey, Loren. *Discipline Without Tyranny*. New York: Hawthorn Books, Inc., 1972.

Herrnstein, R.J. "Measuring Evil." *Commentary*, 1974, June, 57:82.

Hill, Winifred F. *Learning: A Survey Of Psychological Interpretations*. San Francisco, California: Chandler Publishing Co., 1963.

Homan, William E. *Child Sense.* New York: Bantam Books, 1969.

Hunt, J. McV. *Intelligence and Experience.* New York: Ronald, 1961.

Kaufmann, Walter. "Do You Crave A Life Without Choice?" *Psychology Today,* 1973, April, 78ff.

Kelman, Herbert C. and Lee H. Lawrence. "American Response to the Trial of Lt. William L. Calley." *Psychology Today,* 1972, June, 41ff.

Kilpatrick, William. *The Montessori System Examined.* Boston: Houghton Mifflin, 1914.

Kohlberg, Lawrence. "The Child as a Moral Philosopher." *Psychology Today,* 1968, September, 25ff.

Kramer, Rita. "Parent and Child: A Look Back in Wonder." *New York Times Magazine,* 1969a, June 8, 93ff.

Kramer, Rita. "Phasing Out Mom and Dad." *New York Times Magazine,* 1969b, November 2, 95ff.

Lobsenz, Norman M. "What Parents Should Know about Punishing Their Children." *Redbook,* 1972, January, 64ff.

Maslow, Abraham H. *The Farther Reaches of Human Nature.* New York: Viking Press, 1971.

Maw, Wallace H. and Ethel W. Maw. "Selection of Unbalanced and Unusual Designs by Children High in Curiosity."*Child Development,* 1962, December, 33:917-922.

McIntire, Roger W. "Parenthood Training or Mandatory Birth Control: Take Your Choice." *Psychology Today,* 1973, October, 34ff.

Milgram, Stanley. *Obedience to Authority.* New York: Harper & Row, 1974a.

Milgram, Stanley. "The Frozen World of the Familiar Stranger." *Psychology Today*, 1974b, June, 70ff.

Montgomery, K.C. and M. Segall. "Discrimination Learning Based Upon the Exploratory Drive." *Journal Of Physiological Psychology*, 1955, 48:225-228.

Park, Barbara K. "Make Room for Responsibility." *Parents' Magazine*, 1973, October, 38ff.

Piaget, Jean. *The Child's Conception of the World*. New York: Basic Books, 1954.

Piaget, Jean. *Judgment and Reasoning in the Child*. Totowa, New Jersey: Littlefield. Adams & Co., 1959.

Piaget, Jean. *The Moral Judgment of the Child*. New York: Free Press, 1965.

Piaget, Jean. *Play, Dreams, and Imitation in Childhood*. New York: Norton, 1962.

Piaget, Jean. *The Psychology of the Child*. New York: Basic Books, 1969.

Piaget, Jean. *Science of Education and the Psychology of the Child*. New York: Orion Press, 1970.

Piaget, Jean. *Six Psychological Studies*. New York: Random House, 1967.

Powell, Lewis F. Jr. "Eroding Authority." *Vital Speeches*, 1972, October 1, 38:752.

Pritzkau, Philo T. *On Education for the Authentic*. Scranton: International Textbook Co., 1970.

Pulaski, Mary Ann Spencer. *Understanding Piaget: An Introduction to Children's Cognitive Development*. New York: Harper & Row, 1971.

Salk, Lee. "What Decisions Parents Should Allow Children To Make." *Today's Health*, 1973, June, 38-42.

Sarason, Seymour B. *The Culture of the School and the Schools in Change.* Boston: Allyn & Bacon, Inc., 1971.

Shannon Williams V. "Right On! to Responsibility." *Parents' Magazine,* 1973, May, 35ff.

Sharp, Evelyn. *Thinking Is Child's Play.* New York: Avon Books, 1970.

Skinner, B.F. *Walden Two.* New York: Macmillan Paperbacks Edition, 1962.

Slobin, Dan I. "Children and Language: They Learn The Same All Around the World." *Psychology Today,* 1972, July, 82ff.

Smith, Judith and Donald E.P. Smith. "Learning to Tell Right from Wrong." *New York Times Magazine,* 1968 March 3, 90ff.

Smock, Charles D. and Bess G. Holt. "Children's Reactions to Novelty: An Experimental Study of 'Curiosity Motivation.' " *Child Development,* 1962, September, 33:631-642.

Spock, Benjamin. *Baby and Child Care.* New York: Pocket Books, 1946.

Terrell, G. "Manipulation Motivation In Children." *Journal of Psychological Psychology.* 1959, 52:705-709.